The Mystical Initiations of Love

The Path to Self-Mastery, vol 5

The Mystical Initiations of Love

KIM MICHAELS

MORE TO LIFE PUBLISHING

www.morepublish.com

For foreign and translation rights,

contact info@ morepublish.com

ISBN: 978-87-93297-04-3

The information and insights in this book should not be considered as a form of therapy, advice, direction, diagnosis, and/or treatment of any kind. This information is not a substitute for medical, psychological, or other professional advice, counseling and care. All matters pertaining to your individual health should be supervised by a physician or appropriate health-care practitioner. No guarantee is made by the author or the publisher that the practices described in this book will yield successful results for anyone at any time. They are presented for informational purposes only, as the practice and proof rests with the individual.

For more information: *www.ascendedmasterlight.com and www.transcendencetoolbox.com*

CONTENTS

LOVE

INTRODUCTION

This book is part of the series *The Path to Self-Mastery*. The purpose of the series is to give you a complete course for knowing and passing the mystical initiations of the seven spiritual rays. The books in the series form a progression and it is recommended that you start by working through the books to the First Ray of God Power and the Second Ray of God Wisdom before progressing to this book.

The purpose of this book is to teach you about the characteristics of the Third Ray, which will show you how to unlock the flow of unconditional love. If you are new to ascended master teachings, you will benefit greatly from reading the first book in the series, *The Power of Self*, because it gives a general introduction to the spiritual path as it is taught by the ascended masters. This will give you a good foundation for taking greater advantage of the teachings in this book.

This book is designed as a workbook in order to help you better integrate and apply the teachings. You will get the best results if you give the invocation that corresponds to the chapter you are studying. It is recommended that you give a specific invocation once a day for nine days and then study part of the corresponding dictation before or after giving the invocation. Each evening, make calls to be taken to Paul the Venetian's retreat in the etheric realm over Château de Liberté in Southern France.

You give an invocation by reading it aloud, thereby invoking high-frequency spiritual energy. For more information about invocations and how to give them, please see the website: *www.transcendencetoolbox.com*. In order to learn more about the ascended masters and how they give dictations, see the website *www.ascendedmasterlight.com*. If you are not familiar with the concepts of the fall and of fallen beings, please read *Cosmology of Evil*. That books gives a profound yet easily understood explanation of why there are some beings who have no respect for the free will (or lives) of human beings. It explains why they are willing to do anything in order to control us or destroy those who will not be controlled.

1 | INTRODUCING THE THIRD RAY

Color of the Third Ray: Pink
Corresponding chakra: Heart
Elohim: Heros and Amora
Archangel and Archeia: Chamuel and Charity
Chohan: Paul the Venetian
Decrees for the Third Ray: 3.01 Decree to Elohim Heros, 3.02 Decree to Archangel Chamuel, 3.03 Decree to Paul the Venetian.

Pure qualities of the Third Ray

Traditionally, the Third Ray has been seen as the seat of love, compassion, charity, appreciation for beauty and selflessness. A deeper understanding is that the Third Ray is the seat of balance.

Love can be seen as the balancing force in life, the force that balances the two basic forces of creation, namely the outgoing (masculine or Father impulse) and the contracting (feminine or Mother impulse). If these two forces are not balanced, there will be a tendency to take one of them towards the extreme. This means that anything which is created from imbalance will either be taken too far and blow apart. Or it will not be taken far enough whereby it will not come to fruition, eventually self-destructing through contraction.

The pure Third Ray qualities give you the ability to experience unconditionality, namely the one reality that is beyond the two extremes created by the dualistic mind. You can feel when something is dualistic, even though you may not yet have a detailed explanation. You sense that conditionality is not "right," because you experience the unconditional nature of God/reality in your heart.

Third ray qualities lead to a deep inner sense of oneness with all life, which gives rise to the ability to discern when something feels right (because it seeks to raise all life) or feels not right (because it seeks to raise one part of life while putting down another). It is through the Third Ray that you can know what is the right thing to do, even if you cannot yet explain why through the mind. It is also through the Third Ray qualities that you can sense when something is driven by a selfish impulse, and this gives you the power to balance yourself.

Perversions of the Third Ray

The primary perversion of the Third Ray is a lack of balance, but this can be expressed in many subtle ways. One way is what many people call love, but which is really a possessive attempt to control others. In extreme forms, this can be expressed as hatred and the desire to punish or destroy those who refuse to be controlled. For example, many people fall in love but then begin to express a sense of ownership towards the person they claim to love.

Another perversion is the firm belief that the ends can justify the means, meaning that because a person loves this superior cause, it is justified to force or kill other people in order to further the cause. This perverted form of love has caused some of the worst atrocities in human history. Few people are harder to convince than those whose outlook on life is unbalanced by fanaticism. It is what causes people to believe that in order to demonstrate their love for God, they have to kill other people. Killing for a supposedly good cause is an extreme perversion of love.

LOVE

2 | INTRODUCING PAUL THE VENETIAN

In his final embodiment, Paul the Venetian was the Italian renaissance painter Paulo Veronese who lived in Venice for most of his working life. He is especially famous for painting with much brighter, almost transparent, colors than his contemporaries. His aim was to show the higher forms and translucent beauty of the etheric octave, to which he had become attuned already in prior lifetimes. He was then, as now, driven by one simple motivator: a love for beauty. He had a deep belief that beauty is a key ingredient in transforming human beings towards their highest potential.

You may have in your mind the image of artists as eccentric egomaniacs obsessed with fame, but Paul the Venetian will not fit that mold. In his Presence you will sense what it is like to be completely beyond ego, and you feel his deep love for raising all human beings. You also sense a very practical approach, far beyond the dreamers, poets or philosophers. Paul the Venetian is in a sense an idealist, but only because he has proven through his own growth and ascension that love for beauty is a viable pathway to self-transformation. His entire Being radiates this love, and by attuning to his Presence, you will begin to receive his visions of higher beauty—the mere sight of which will transform your consciousness.

Paul the Venetian is not a teacher who primarily uses words to teach. He discourses through images that he has learned to convey directly to the minds of receptive students. For those less receptive, his retreat contains rooms with large 360 degree displays upon which students watch images of transforming beauty—until they are transformed enough to attune to Paul directly. New students often have many questions, but Paul's typical response is: "Let us look at some pictures and then we will see how many of your questions remain." He then displays images designed specifically for each student, and by the time the display is over, the questions suddenly seem irrelevant or have simply been forgotten.

Even in his etheric retreat, Paul the Venetian can seem ethereal, as he plays a kind of hide-and-seek with new students, those whose minds are still so attuned to the ugliness of human creation that they have a hard time even seeing ethereal forms. To such students, Paul can appear almost ghostly, as if they cannot keep their eye focused upon him because he seems to be constantly going in and out of view.

As students learn to raise their attunement, so they no longer focus on the ugly but instead focus on the beautiful, they will begin to see Paul the Venetian clearly. They will sense the pink emanation of love from his heart chakra, a pinkness laced with sparkles of ruby fire. This ruby fire makes Paul immovable while still seeming completely loving and gentle. Try to project manifestations of ugliness at him, and you will find them consumed before they can even reach the core of his auric sheath. You will never get him to react to the ugly, as his oneness with Divine beauty is such that nothing ugly can even make an impression.

Paul the Venetian's greatest ability is to help people raise their sights towards a higher vision. They might start seeing beauty in nature, then in the etheric realm and then perhaps even in Paul himself. The end goal is that the students start seeing the beauty within themselves. Paul never loses sight of the beauty within you. He continues to hold this immaculate vision for you until you yourself can no longer deny the beauty of God's creation in you.

LOVE

3 | EXPRESSING THE IMMEASURABLE

Paul the Venetian. What is in a name? Only what you put there. The Third Ray of Love. What is in love? Only what you put there. What is in a work of art? Only what you put there—unless you have become an open door for the stream of the creative fount of love to be expressed through your art or through your daily life.

Shall we not realize that art has become, as almost everything else touched by man, a concept that people seek to *understand*. Shall we not realize that when people seek to understand based on the mind that is steeped in separation and duality, what they understand is not true art or true love. It is only what they put there, or what has been put there by other beings steeped in duality.

So much of the art in the world is adapted to a certain time period, to a certain culture, to a certain view of what *is* and what *is not* art. In some cases it has a certain overlay, such as what was imposed by the Inquisition, of what was acceptable and not acceptable to put in a painting. Or a certain political regime, such as the Soviet Union, might have imposed an overlay for what was considered the true art of the socialist utopia.

True art cannot be expressed within the framework of a certain man–made mental box. True art is ever–transcending. It is creative but not as you normally understand creativity, for even creativity has become a concept upon which human beings project their mental images of what it means to be creative. You cannot say what it means to be creative, for creativity is that which transcends boundaries, even the boundaries of what has been expressed before.

The Chateau de Liberté

Some of you will know that I am the hierarch at the retreat called the Château de Liberté. You will know that it is located in the etheric realm over a certain physical location in France. You might even know that there is a physical castle and that this castle has a certain look, a certain design. You might do what human beings are so good at doing: take their own mental images and project it upon that which is beyond the physical. Look at how people throughout history have projected their own mental images upon God.

When you see pictures of the building of the Château in France, you might think that my etheric retreat looks somewhat like that building. Think again, my beloved, for in the etheric realm things are not solidified as they are in the physical. When you take a great amount of rocks or stones and start stacking them on top of each other in order to build a building that will stand for a long time, then you obviously create a matrix in the physical. It will not easily be broken down and will not easily be changed, for what are you in essence doing? When you set out to build a building that will stand for a long time, what is it that wants to build that building? It is the ego that wants to create a monument to itself that will stand for a long time, longer than the physical body through which it is expressing itself and which it knows has a short lifespan.

So many things in the world are simply an attempt of human egos to immortalize themselves. When you look at the art world, you likewise see so many of these attempts of the artist, or the person commissioning the artist, to immortalize their egos. Take for example one of the monumental paintings of the inauguration ceremony of Napoleon Bonaparte and you will see exactly what I mean. A gigantic painting painted for the sole purpose of immortalizing the ego of Napoleon. Given that my retreat is located in the etheric octave over France, you will see that France, as a nation, has a certain tendency to want to immortalize certain aspects of its national ego. Of course, this is not limited to France, as many other nations have the exact same tendency. They want to raise monuments to themselves that can stand for a long time and be recognized and admired as, so to speak, great works of art. *Are* they great works of arts?

Artists setting monuments to themselves

What, truly, is a work of art? Is not an act of kindness a true work of art? Is not the true artist one who does not desire to set a monument to himself or herself. True artists are content in being part of the ever–flowing stream of life, playing a little part in redirecting that stream, making it flow into a more positive, more beautiful expression and then simply moving on.

My beloved, at my retreat, students are meant to learn about love. You may think that we have classrooms where we sit people down at a desk and then I or another master stands up at the pulpit or at the blackboard and we start giving a lecture about love. If you will think about this with the heart, you will realize that there is a fundamental problem. How do you teach people about love? How can you come to *understand* love? This is a question to ponder, for many of you have never pondered it before. Even though we have sometimes talked about unconditional love and you may have read about unconditional love, you have not sat down and seriously pondered it. How can you *understand* unconditional love, how can you capture that which is unconditional, that which is immeasurable? It is not possible. Just as you cannot easily quantify what is good art, you cannot quantify what is true love.

The path has several stages. The reason it is important to understand this is that you then realize that what serves you well at a particular stage will not help you transcend that stage. It can often become a crutch that prevents you from walking onto the next level of the path.

The spiritual rays are not separated

There are seven rays, and what is it important to understand about the seven rays, my beloved? So many times we see our students get this idea that the rays are somehow separated. You can take one after the other. You study the one and you master the one, and then you move on to the next and you move on to the next. Many times you do not fully see that behind the seven rays – even though they *can* be separated – there is a deeper flow of life, a flow of creativity.

What are the seven rays? The purpose of the seven rays is to free your creative powers from any limitation put upon them. This might be a limitation put upon you from the outside, from the society in which you have grown up, even from the collective consciousness of the earth. It might be a limitation put upon you from the inside, from your own beliefs, the things you take for granted and never question.

It is all well and good to gain a certain mastery on the First Ray. If you then fall in love with yourself as having the mastery of the First Ray, then how can you lay down that life of the First Ray, lay down the mastery gathered on the First Ray, in order to follow Christ when he beckons you to move on to the Second Ray? So again with the Second Ray. It is all well and good to seek wisdom, to seek understanding, on the Second Ray, but what good will that understanding do you when you come to my retreat on the Third Ray? Now you think you have to transfer your mastery from the Second Ray so that you will quickly use that mastery to understand the Third Ray. My beloved, *it cannot be done!*

What is there to *understand* about love? It either flows or it doesn't flow. If you are not willing to let it flow, then all of the understanding in the world will not unlock your heart and create an opening for the flow of life that wants to be expressed through you.

What are we to do with some of the many students, especially in this modern age, who come in here with their well-developed rational, linear minds? They come in eager, just as you see the most eager students in the earthly schools. They are ready with their notebooks, they sit there ready to take notes of everything that the teacher says about love. They want to build up this intellectual, linear, rational understanding of love. They think this will get them the highest grade in the class.

What are we to do with such students? We do not wish to discourage anyone. If we try to tell them how limited their view of love is, they will often be discouraged. They are so focused on this momentum of understanding, that they do not know what to do with themselves if there is something they cannot understand. Then they will suddenly begin to judge themselves based on their momentum of understanding and they will think: "But if I can't understand love, there must be something wrong with me. I must be deficient and therefore I am not as good of a student as I thought." This is not what we desire so what do we do?

The challenge for new students

There are many rooms in my retreat, my beloved, many rooms. If you take what I said before about the etheric retreats being different from earthly buildings, you might realize that my retreat is always expanding, it is always transcending itself. It has a different design today than it had thirty years ago, for I have expanded the design.

What is an etheric retreat? Is it a building that is set in stone as you see an earthly building? Nay, it is not. It is an image projected onto the screen of the Ma-ter Light in the etheric realm by the master who is the hierarch for the retreat and by those who serve as his helpers in that retreat.

When we receive a new student, we are able to expand the retreat and project a certain environment that this student might need in order to move on. Many of the students will need some time when they experience an environment like a kindergarten on earth. The students are given paint or clay and allowed to do anything they want, express themselves in any way they want without any restrictions or judgments whatsoever. This goes on until these students learn one thing: To express themselves without judging but simply for the pure love of expressing their creativity.

This is not about producing a physical work of art. People will be in these settings until they realize that it is the process that is important, not the end result. After they have had their focus on results softened up, we will put some of our students through a special test.

We will tell them that their next task is to paint a portrait of themselves as they look in their full Christhood. We will give them an atelier designed with each person in mind. On the walls of that atelier will be scenes from that person's past lives, some of the things to which this person is particularly attached, even if they were not aware of this consciously during their present or latest lifetime. They will sit there in this environment where they are constantly reminded about their past and they will be asked to paint a portrait of themselves as they look in their Christhood.

Many of the most eager students will immediately begin to paint this portrait based on how they look in their etheric form. When you come to a retreat and have not graduated from that retreat, even your etheric form, even your sense of identity, is affected by the many experiences you have had on earth. That is precisely why your etheric look will be affected by the scenes on the walls from your past lifetimes.

We will allow a student as much time as that student desires to paint this portrait. When it is done, when the student feels it is done, then I and others will come to critique the portrait. We will not critique it as you might think on earth, as a panel of judges that you see in these talent competitions where the three judges sit there and now they have to make some kind of funny remark on television. They sometimes make remarks that are certainly not helpful to the creative progress of the student but are an expression of the ego of the judge.

We do not critique in this way. We can take the student through a meditation where the student sees the portrait not based on the state of consciousness through which it painted the portrait, but it is temporarily taken out of that state of consciousness and sees the portrait with the light of Christ. Then it has a glimpse where it has the opportunity to see the limitations incorporated into the portrait.

Erasing the records from the past

After having given a student this experience, we will again leave the student and say: "Now continue to paint on the portrait until you feel it is right." What will usually happen is that the student, after seeing a glimpse of the Christ consciousness, will realize how the portrait was affected by a certain experience from its past. Instead of immediately starting to repaint the portrait, the person will take some white paint and it will paint over one of the scenes on the walls of the atelier. It will then use all of the spiritual tools we have, including the Violet Flame, to erase that record from its past. The student will continue until the record is so thoroughly erased that it no longer affects its etheric body and therefore is no longer part of its identity.

When the student has erased the record, it will go back, take one look at the portrait, and it will realize it cannot possibly be changed because that etheric record was so ingrained that it affected every aspect of the looks. The student must do what it did to the wall: start with a new white canvas and paint over. When the old record is erased, your etheric image will look different than it did before. This is a process that can continue many times. In the end there may come a situation where a student has now painted a portrait of himself that is not affected by any of the records that it has from any lifetime on earth.

The portrait of true Christhood

We are now called into the atelier, and the atelier has completely white walls. In the center of a white room is the portrait, and then we can give the student praise and say: "Truly, you have painted yourself without any human records, but now is this portrait really you as you look in the fullness of your Christhood?" Then we simply leave this person with one last thought: "We want you to make sure that the portrait you paint, the portrait you leave, is the one you want to preserve for posterity as an accurate and complete record of yourself in the fullness of your Christhood." Then we leave the student with this thought.

In many cases, we will be called back, for now the student has painted a new portrait. Sometimes students will have to go through this experience a number of times. Sometimes a student gets it the very first time. It takes this beautiful etheric portrait that it has painted and it contemplates what it means to be in the fullness of your Christhood. Then it calls us back.

We are called back into an atelier that has completely white walls and in the center is the painting. The painting is also completely white and then the student says: "I realized that there is no such thing as the fullness of my Christhood. When I am in Christhood, I am constantly flowing with the ever-bubbling fount of the love of God that constantly breaks all conditions. Attempting to paint a portrait of myself in the fullness of my Christhood, a portrait that I want to preserve for posterity, would simply be like taking a snapshot of a river. Obviously, a still frame can never capture the fullness of the flowing river. I have no longer any desire to sit here in this room and try to paint a portrait of my Christhood. Instead, I desire to go out on the highways and byways of life and express that Christhood by seeking to help others transcend their limitations."

Expressing the immeasurable

My beloved, this is when we sometimes shed a tear, for this student has truly captured the fullness of the Third Ray of Love. We simply smile and we look at the student, the student looks at us and there are no words to be said. We know – we *experience* – the fullness of our Christhood as it is at that moment. There is a certain joy, a certain bubbling love, when two beings who have reached a certain level of Christhood meet and they look at each other and acknowledge each others Christhood—and nothing else is needed.

The student goes out and now it can begin to express a greater fullness of the Third Ray of Love, this unconditional, immeasurable, unquantifiable love. Those who are the good students on the First and the Second Ray have often come to want to measure their attainment and their progress. On the

First and the Second Ray, this can to some degree be done by measuring how much power you can express, how much wisdom you have, how much understanding of certain concepts you have. On the Third Ray of Love, how can you measure your progress in expressing the immeasurable, that which cannot be quantified? As long as you want to *quantify* love, you are not flowing with love. You must sit there and continue to try to capture a still frame of the ever–moving river of love.

The important point is that you go beyond *understanding* love, beyond wanting to quantify love and measure love but you now *experience* the flow of love. This is my gift. Paul the Venetian I AM. I bid you adieu from the Château de Liberté in the etheric plane. I bid you flow with the Love that I AM.

4 | LOVE AND POWER

I AM the Ascended Master Paul the Venetian. I AM the Chohan of the Third Ray that has normally been called the ray of love.

It is my aim for this series of discourses to continue the work we have begun of exposing to the people in embodiment the initiations that you face under the seven Chohans. These initiations are geared towards helping you build the momentum that takes you to the 96th level of consciousness. It also takes you beyond that level so that you pass the initiation where you truly begin the path of Christhood, rather than falling down, using your creative powers to build the ego.

The physical and the personal journey

My retreat is located over the South of France. It is called the Château de Liberté, which is the building that is the focus for the retreat in the physical. There is nothing wrong with traveling to the physical place where one of our retreats is located, but you do need to remember that the retreat is located in the etheric realm. That means you have to tune in to a higher level of vibration than the physical. If you can do so better by going to the physical place, this is perfectly fine, but you do not *have* to go to the physical place in order to tune in to the vibration. It must be said that there are many times when people have to make a physical journey in order to make the corresponding journey in consciousness.

This is the whole idea depicted in the legend of Odysseus who made the Odyssey. This epic journey was a symbol for his journey in consciousness, confronting his own internal momentums, or his internal spirits, as we call it today. You, too, are engaged in such a journey. It may never be written about in poetic form, it may never be known by anyone but yourself, but it is a journey of some importance. I will not say *epic* importance because we have given you teachings about the epic mindset [See *Freedom from Ego Dramas*]. It is an important journey, not only for you personally but because you are carving a trail in the collective consciousness that makes it easier for others to walk the path.

The Conscious You is always flowing

Do not overlook this, for one of the greatest dangers on the path is this sense of discouragement, the sense that you are beginning to become used to walking the path, used to following the instructions of the ascended masters. You may become used to a certain level of consciousness. It is not *you* who become used to anything. It is your *ego* who becomes used to something.

The core of your being is what we have called the Conscious You. It is created out of the Creator's Being, and the Creator's Being, regardless of the images you may have in your mind, is not standing still. It is the ever-flowing stream of life. Your Conscious You is never standing still but is always flowing. Your ego is what wants to stop the passage of time, stop the physical universe, so that it feels it has life under control. When your Conscious You identifies itself with the ego, then you think you have a need to be in control. You even think you have a need to be in control of your path. When you come to the initiations at our retreat, you come with a certain preoccupied opinion about who you are, who we are as the ascended masters and what the path of initiation should be like. Do you understand that the danger of giving you an outer teaching is precisely that you form a mental image of how we should teach you? What have we said over and over again? What keeps you trapped in the material universe is your mental images, your sense of how the world works, how God is and how you are. You need to transcend those images! You need to go beyond them! How can we help you go beyond your mental image of us and our teaching if we conform to it, thereby validating the image, keeping you trapped in it?

This is what the false hierarchy will do. They will tell you: "You are right. You now have the highest teaching on the planet. You just need to continue doing this for the rest of your life and you will be guaranteed to qualify for your ascension." They tell you this because they want to sabotage your ascension, and the best way to do this – they know – is to keep you clinging to some aspect of the ego and the sense that you are in control.

Do you know how many people have found the ascended masters' teachings over the last century and who felt that now they have arrived. Now they have come home; now they have found the highest teaching on the planet, the teaching that will take them to the ascension. They have then used the teaching to reinforce their ego's sense of being in control. They have felt that now that they have this outer teaching and this outer set of practices, they are in control of their path.

My beloved, if you want to be in control of your path, then you do not need the ascended masters, do you? You need a graven image of the ascended masters, which you keep affirming as the real thing. Then I cannot help you. No ascended master can help you. You cannot even enter my retreat of the Third Ray if you hold on to these mental images.

The image that you need to be willing to shatter as the first step on the initiations under me is your image of love. If you are willing to, in some measure, transcend your mental images, then you can enter my retreat.

I can assure you that you cannot graduate from Lanto's retreat, unless you show some willingness to transcend your mental images. I am giving this warning at the beginning of this book because there are those who may start reading this book as the first one without going through the two previous books.

I am not hereby saying that there cannot be people who have already passed the initiations of the first two rays, and are ready for the initiations of the Third Ray without reading the other two books. They have passed these initiations at inner levels, but there are few of those. It would be wise to be humble and go through the first two books before you engage in this one, but if you do have a strong inner sense that you are ready for this book, then I will not discourage you. Make sure that this sense comes from within, and not from the ego's pride of wanting to show that you are an advanced student and that you are ready for the initiations of love.

The initiation of Love and Power

What happens when people enter my retreat? The first initiation they face is the initiation of love combined with the First Ray of Power. This is one of the most difficult initiations for people who have embodied on this planet for a long time. There is hardly any concept that has been more misunderstood and misused than love. As we have explained, everything on earth can be said to revolve around a power game [See *Freedom from Ego Games*]. This is the essence of the ego, the desire to establish a sense of being in control by overpowering other people, physical conditions on the planet or even the ascended masters or God.

What is it that the fallen beings have been trying to accomplish since the original fall, which happened so long ago measured with earth time that it is unfathomable to the outer mind? They have been trying to establish control over God. They use all means to do this, including love. How can you use love to control? Just look at planet earth and the interactions of human beings, their so-called love relationships.

Presenting the initiations of love

When you come to my retreat, most people are so convinced that they already know what love is, what it is not, how it should be expressed, and how it should not be expressed. They are also relatively convinced that, as ascended master students who have some experience with the path, they have a good idea of what kind of initiations I should give them. This we need to overcome as the very first step. I cannot initiate you on the path of love if you are seeking to use your image of love to overpower me. I am the teacher; you are the student. I have passed the initiations of love. Therefore, I am presenting those initiations to you. It is not the other way around.

It is often shocking for students to find that, when they come to my retreat, I am not the gentle master that they come to expect from a master of love. This is not to say that I am not gentle, but I am not in the beginning when I give you the initiations of the Third Ray. I am unbending, unyielding and uncompromising.

Many students feel that I am using power against them, that I am seeking to overpower them. I am not. I am only mirroring back what they are sending at me, and most students come here projecting their misunderstood concept of love as a disguised power game. This is not said as a form of blame. You can hardly grow up on this planet without being programmed to play this power game through love. This power game is so common, so pervasive, on this planet that it is virtually impossible to grow up here without being affected by it.

The sternness of my voice does not mean that I do not accept you. It just means that I need to reflect back what you are sending at me and also to demonstrate that, no matter what power game you think you are playing, it has no effect on me. You will not trick me into letting you overpower me, and you will not overpower me through raw force alone. Nor will you do it with a velvet glove of the soft aspect of love.

I have passed the initiations of love. There is nothing you can take with you from earth that can fool or force me into submitting to your power game. I cannot free you from the game by submitting to it, can I? Nor, for that matter, can I free you from it by opposing you and seeking to overpower you. What I *can* do is demonstrate that I cannot be moved, that I will not be moved, that I am immovable by any power game on earth—no matter how cleverly disguised as love.

When students have overcome their initial shock of being met with this very different master than they had imagined, then we can take the next step. Because the people who come here have already gone through the initiations of the two first rays, it is relatively easy for them to make the switch. It can be a little harder for you in the outer mind. I am giving you this teaching in a way that your outer mind can read so that you may contemplate it with the outer mind. If you are reading this book and continuing to read this book, then you have most likely already made this shift at the inner. You just need to let it filter through to the outer mind so that you have that outer willingness to begin to look at life on earth and look at how people use love in their power games with each other.

The next step we take at my retreat is that we take the students into a room where we have what you would call a technological device. You have heard the other Chohans talk about such rooms with different devices. In mine, we have an instrument that is specifically attuned to detect love, the vibrations of the Third Ray. What we can show on this instrument is a visual form of how people use the energy of the Third Ray. When I say the energies of the Third Ray, I mean not only pure love but also the perversions of love. We can make visible to students what energies they have in their own energy fields that are a perversion of love. Most students are not even aware that these are perversions. Most people on earth are not aware of how love has been perverted, but we can make this visual.

We can show specific situations of how the students have interacted with other people, or how people in general interact with each other. We can even go back in time and show them specific situations from history where famous people in important events in world history have interacted. We can show how they have used a perverted form of love and how the energy was flowing between them. We can show how one person had a reservoir of the perverted love energies in his or her consciousness and was then directing it into the subconscious mind of other people where it eventually had the effect of overpowering or persuading them. The people were overpowered or persuaded into accepting that this perversion of love was actually love.

Perversions of the energies of the Third Ray

Most people on earth do not understand how they have perverted love, and what is the reason for this? It is that the perversions of love are what they identify as love. They think that the perversions of the energies of the Third Ray are true love, real love. It is a shock for people to see in a visual form how the energies have been taken below the vibration of pure love, how they have been named as real love, and then to see how they are used in various power games to control other people.

This is often a rude awakening, and it is fortunate that it happens in the retreat of love. When we have shaken the student out of its blindness of thinking false love is true love, we can then let the student experience true love, and *that* is the healer of the shock of seeing anti-love. Anti-love is probably the most cleverly disguised perversion found on this planet because so many people have such a desire for love, to be loving, to be loved. They are so reluctant to give up their images of what they think is true love, what they have been conditioned to see as true love, what they have been programmed to accept as true love.

Most of the students who come to my retreat, having gone through the initiations of the First Ray, have risen above the most obvious perversions of love. Otherwise, they could not have climbed beyond the 48th level. They often see themselves as loving or at least non-violent, non-aggressive people—and they *are*. They have made progress. If you are reading this, you have made progress in terms of rising above the more obvious perversions of love. Be careful to realize that if you had passed the initiations of love, you would not be at my retreat. You still have some perversions of love, only it is now the more cleverly disguised ones that you are facing.

Perversions in love relationships

What we start out showing students in the retreat are the more obvious perversions of love. This is what you see among people who are below the 48th level, which is the case for most people on earth. You might even take a look at your own life and see if there are not people you know who are in a so-called love relationship but who have some obvious perversions. Do you know someone where the man and the woman are engaged in a constant power game, seeking to establish some form of dominance? Do you know someone where one of the partners has already established dominance and the other one has submitted to this?

They may seem to live a harmonious and peaceful relationship because one person has obtained the dominance that the person desires and the other one has submitted to it. You may see people who live that way for twenty, thirty, forty years or more in a marriage, but are they growing from that experience? Nay, they are not. Are you growing from the experience of being locked in a constant battle of arguing or bickering with your partner? Nay, you are not.

Take a look at the relationship between parents and children. How many of you have had a controlling parent who attempted to control you for various reasons? It may be that your parent wanted you to outlive his or her own unfulfilled life, have the education, do the things that they could never do. It may be that they just want to keep you down so that you do not become better than them. Some parents want their children to become better than they are, and other parents do not want them to even become equal. They want to keep their children down. Either way can be a perversion of love, if the parent is seeking to force the child rather than allowing the child to discover who it is, to discover its Divine plan and to express that rather than some human expectation or matrix put upon it by the parent.

How many mothers, for instance, have felt that – because they bore the child in their womb, gave birth to the child in a painful process, sacrificed their life or even their career to raise the child – the child owes something to the mother? In most cases where the mother feels this, the deeper reality is that the mother had severe karma with the lifestream of the child from past lives. Giving birth to that child and raising it was the only opportunity that the mother had for balancing that karma. How does the child owe anything to the mother when the child has given the mother an opportunity to balance her karma? How does your child owe you anything when you have received an opportunity to be free? Will you be free by feeling that your child owes you something? Nay, you will not. You will reinforce the pattern that caused you to make the karma so long ago. How long, O Lord, will these people continue these power games where they claim to love someone, but they are only seeking to control them at subconscious levels?

Using love to argue and control

When I tell you these things, you may experience that your outer mind will argue against my words. A substantial portion of the people who read this will notice that their outer minds are coming up with questions or arguments. I do not intend to comment on the particular questions or arguments. What I want you to become aware of is the process.

I want you to become aware that it is your outer mind who is questioning, who is arguing, who is seeking to deny or refute my words. Why do you think your outer mind is attempting to get you to deny the words that are only geared towards setting you free? It is because your outer mind is playing a control game with *you*. If you like playing this control game with your own outer mind, I have no objection. The Law of Free Will gives you the right to do this, but then I must question what use you have of being at my retreat. Are you ready for the initiation of love and power? Are you ready to see how subtle the ego can be in using love?

Most people who come to my retreat can easily see how people who are below the 48th level of consciousness are using love in order to gain control over others. Most of you have actually been exposed to this from a parent or from other significant people in your life, such as spouses, siblings, bosses at work or whatever it may be. Many of you have seen these abuses of power all your life.

Some of you have rebelled against them and gotten yourself into various unpleasant situations as a result. Those who play a power game do not like to be challenged, do they? What will they always do? They will go after *you* on a very personal level. They will feel that you are trying to destroy their power, and in return, they will use their power to destroy *you*. Such is one of the oldest games played on planet earth.

What is behind a power game? Why are you seeking control? It is because you fear something. You fear loss. The ultimate perversion, or the *first* perversion, of love is fear. What is it you fear? When you are in love, when you are in the flow of the energies of love, there is no fear, but why is that so? Because you know, you *experience,* that love is always flowing. How can you lose if you are always flowing? Think about this, my beloved. Think about it, in so many ways in your life.

Recognizing the standstill of the ego

Imagine in the old days where you had this technology called a video recorder or a video player. You could put a cassette into the player and you could play a movie on your television. The tape was moving inside the player, but sometimes it might stop or it might freeze and then the movie would stand still. My beloved, when you are watching a movie and it suddenly stands still, do you not instantly recognize that something has gone wrong here? If you are riding a train and it suddenly stops in the middle of the tracks, do you not realize that something has gone wrong? If you are flying an airplane and it suddenly stops, you will certainly know that something has gone wrong, for what will happen to an airplane that stops moving forward? It will start moving downward and very quickly.

Movement is the nature of the Conscious You; stillstand is the nature of the ego. The Conscious You does not feel fear as long as it is moving, but when it steps into the ego, it gains an almost visual, but certainly a sensory, experience that things can stand still, that a certain condition can be maintained over time. Now, it begins to identify with the ego's desire for control through ownership. The ego wants to own because it thinks that if it owns something, it can control that something or that someone.

The perversion of Love and Power

What is the perversion of love on the First Ray of Power? It is ownership, the very concept that you can own something on earth. You do understand, as we have explained many times, that the earth is in an unascended sphere. The earth is one of the lower planets in your sphere, and the earth has been designated as a planet for people at a certain level of consciousness. This is a level where they have gone quite far into separation. When people have gone so far into separation, they cannot instantly come up and out of that state of separation. They cannot make this in one leap, in one jump. It is too big of a distance.

When people have gone so far into separation, they are afraid of movement. They do not find joy in movement. They fear it, and this means that the earth has been designed as a planet where you can actually have the sense of owning something. This does not mean that we of the ascended masters condone ownership, but it means that we use it as a device for helping people have the experience that they own something. Over time, they can have had enough of it, and now they are ready to move on to a higher experience.

Ownership does not come from the spiritual realm. You may say: "But Paul the Venetian, you have a retreat. Do you not own your retreat?" Nay, I do not. It is not, so to speak, *my* retreat, in the sense that you use the word "my." I am the master who is right now the leader of this retreat, but I did not create the retreat. It was created long before I ascended. There will be another master at some point, perhaps one of you walking this path, who will take over this retreat in the future and I will move on. In the ascended realm, you own nothing because you have become one with the River of Life and you realize that there is no stillstand in the river. You have no desire to stand still.

Take a person who falls into a fast-moving river. What will most people seek to do? They will seek to grab on to something that stands still—a rock in the stream, a branch hanging from a tree. They will seek to swim to the shore so that they can get out of the moving river. What is the alternative? It is to realize that the river is not your enemy and that flowing with the river can be enjoyable. Look at how many people like to get in a small boat or a raft and sail down the river. They feel it is fun to ride the river, but why is that? Because they are sitting in a boat that they think they own and that they think they can control. Ownership makes it possible for people at a certain level of consciousness to still somewhat flow with the River of Life but feel they are in control.

Questioning the sense of ownership

Do you begin to see the very delicate situation I face when you come to me at my retreat? I know that you have grown up on planet earth. You have probably embodied here during many lifetimes. I know that your consciousness is affected by this desire to own, to be in control. I know that, so far on your spiritual path under the two previous rays, you have had a sense that you had some degree of control over your path. Master MORE and Lord Lanto have allowed you to maintain a certain level of this sense that you are still in control, even though some of their initiations have shocked you. You, or rather, your ego still has a sense that it is in control of the path.

When you come to my retreat, the first initiation you will face is that you need to begin to question this sense of ownership, of control, the sense of where your path is or should be going, the sense that you are allowing me to guide you but you are still in control. My beloved, I *am* guiding you, but I am guiding *you*, the Conscious You, to be in control and not your ego. That means I must guide you to go beyond the control of the ego by challenging that sense of control.

How some students resist the initiations

Most students who come to my retreat will resist this. Some will resist it violently. Some will leave, at least for a time. There is a certain portion of students who come here, are shown how they subconsciously abuse love energy in their control games, and who get so shocked that they revert back into the control game. They refuse to give it up, argue that I am wrong, that I cannot be a true master if I am not loving, that I cannot be the Chohan of the Third Ray if I am not loving.

They leave in a huff and go back into their egos. They often have no conscious recollection of this, but they sometimes have a strong desire to argue against some condition on earth, against other people. There are even those who have come here and have been so shocked that they have rejected all spirituality for a time. Some of the people who most vehemently reject religion and argue against religion have refused to face the initiation that is the first initiation at my retreat.

You, who are reading or hearing this, may notice that your ego is arguing, is reacting, is finding it shocking that the Chohan of the Third Ray could be so rude, so forceful—as your ego will see it. What you can potentially realize is that what the ego sees is not what *is*. The ego sees a reflection of what it is projecting into the mirror.

What is the key to beginning to become aware of these power games where people use love in order to establish ownership and control? It is to realize that what you experience from the world is not independent of your own mind. What you feel is coming at you, and which your ego tells you is coming from the world or other people, is actually a reflection of what you are sending out at subconscious levels.

Relationships dominated by power games

There are those who play an obvious power game where they want to use the energies of the First Ray to overpower other people and force them into submission. This is not the way you play a power game where you use the perversions of love. When you are using the perversions of love as a power game, you think you are being loving.

You think that what you are sending out is love. When something comes back at you that is not love, you think it is because these other people are not loving, or this master who claims to be the Chohan of the Third Ray is not loving or God is not loving. It is the ego, *your* ego, that is not loving. It claims to be loving. It creates an appearance of being loving, but it is not true love. It is a perversion, one of the perversions that are so common on this earth and that most people have been programmed to think represent true love.

I would venture to say that more than 90 percent of the so-called love relationships you see on this earth are completely dominated by a perversion of love. I mentioned a parent claiming to love a child but wanting to decide how the child should live its life. The parent thinks that it is doing this because it is wiser than the child and knows how the child should live its life in order to be happy or in order to avoid this or that calamity. The parent thinks this is love. There are even children who submit to this because they think it is love. I am not hereby saying you should not take the advice or the counsel of your parents. You should use it only as a way to go within and get an inner sense of whether this is right or not, whether you should follow this or not, or whether you should take your life in a different direction.

Responsibility, response-ability, to your Divine plan

You have a Divine plan that is not the same as that of your parents, your spouse or your children. You have a right to tune in to that plan and follow it, regardless of what these other people want from you. I am not saying you do not have responsibility towards other people, but do you see that even the sense that you have a responsibility towards others is being used in the control game? You *do* have a responsibility towards the children you have brought into this world. You have a responsibility to give them the best possible start in life, but does that mean you have to stop your own Divine plan for the sake of your children? It does not!

Those children volunteered to be born by you, knowing at inner levels who you are and what your Divine plan is. Those children volunteered, at the higher levels of their minds, to come into that situation because they knew it was a growth opportunity for them. It may be that you do something that you know is part of your Divine plan, but your children do not agree with this with their outer minds. They rebel against it, they accuse you and they say you were not a responsible parent. Or you do something that you know is your Divine plan, but it shocks your parents and they say you are not a responsible child. Or you do something that surprises your spouse and your spouse says you are not a responsible partner.

What does the word "responsibility" mean? It means "response-ability." This has an Alpha and an Omega aspect. The Alpha aspect is that you are able to respond when your I AM Presence releases the matrix for a new phase of your Divine plan. If this phase requires you to make some outer changes in your life, then you are able to respond to that. The Omega aspect is that you do the best you can to take care of your worldly situation, including other people. Being response-able in the Omega aspect does not mean that you override your ability to respond to the Alpha. Alpha comes before Omega; it is not the other way around.

Demanding that Spirit should conform to matter

This is the satanic consciousness that Jesus addressed when he told Peter: "Get thee behind me, Satan." You do not demand that Spirit should conform to matter; this is the satanic consciousness. Life on this planet has created so many of these beliefs that if you are a responsible child, parent, spouse or employee, then you are supposed to let your Spirit conform to the demands of the material world.

This does not get you above the 48th level of consciousness. There are many people below the 48th level of consciousness who are not aggressive or evil or what you would call power people. Many of them have submitted to this consciousness that they are supposed to allow their Spirit to conform to matter, and that is why they cannot go beyond the 48th level. They have overcome aggression. They have overcome what you normally call evil tendencies, even egotistical tendencies, but they cannot engage the path precisely because they still believe that they need to allow their Spirit to conform to matter.

Do you understand, my beloved? The path of self-mastery that we are teaching in this course is a path where you stop allowing your Spirit to conform to matter. You become response-able to flow with the Spirit. This does not mean that you ignore or set aside your worldly responsibilities. It does not mean you suddenly pack up and leave whatever situation you are in, although it *may* require you to do this, as demonstrated by both Jesus and Buddha. It does not necessarily mean this; it is an individual situation. It is perfectly possible to live in a normal, family relationship and walk the path of initiation. This *does* mean that you set your priorities straight so you see that responding to Spirit is your primary responsibility. Then responding to matter happens within the framework of Spirit, within the framework of your Divine plan.

I can assure you that the best way to be a responsible child, parent or spouse is to follow your Divine plan. If your parents, spouse, or children can accept this, then you can have a much higher relationship with them than if they do not. If they do not accept your Divine plan, what kind of relationship will you have? You will have a relationship dominated by the power game where you are submitting to them. You are submitting to their ownership and their control, thereby setting aside or aborting your Divine plan. You understand that no person on earth has the right to demand that another person sets aside or ignores their Divine plan for your sake? This is not a right you have.

Overcoming the game of submissive love

How will you overcome this entire consciousness of using the perversions of love in order to establish ownership and control of other people? The one aspect is that you have to stop using love so that you can gain ownership and control of other people. Because you have already risen through the initiations of Master MORE and Lanto, you have already overcome this to a large extent.

What you face on the Third Ray is this feeling in you that you have to submit to the demands of other people. The majority of the people come to my retreat with this sense: "I am a spiritual person. As a spiritual person, I am supposed to be loving. If I am really loving, I am supposed to be submissive, responsive, to the needs, desires and demands of other people. First of all, I must not do something that causes other people to accuse me of not being loving."

Can you honestly look at your life and see that you have not been caught in this game? Can you look at your life and see how you have had this tendency where you would almost bend over backwards, as they say, in order to avoid other people accusing you of not being loving, not being kind, not being a good person, a good child, a good parent or a good spouse? Can you see that many of you have this fear of being accused of not being loving?

Do you know where this fear comes from? It comes from your ego playing a power game on *you*. It is trying to own you by making you think you have to submit to this worldly image of what it means to be a loving person. The worst thing that could happen to you was that you failed to live up to this image. When you believe this trick of your ego, what are you saying to me, Paul the Venetian, the Chohan of the Third Ray? You are saying: "Master Paul, don't challenge this image that my ego has created. Don't make me do something that makes me susceptible to the accusation that I am not a loving person. Don't make me shock my parents, spouse, children or other people. Don't cause me to do or say something that makes them accuse me of not being loving. I cannot bear this."

Unresolved psychology and accusations from others

How can I help you come up higher? How can I help you pass the first initiation at my retreat? Do you not see that other people accusing you *may* or *may not* have anything to do with *you?* It may be that what they accuse you of is based on a correct observation of some unresolved psychology you have. It may also be that their accusation of you has nothing to do with you. It comes from *their* unresolved psychology that they are projecting at you. This you need to grasp in order to free yourself from these power games that people are playing on you.

I know very well that this is a delicate balance. You cannot say: "Anytime people accuse me, it is because they are projecting their unresolved psychology at me so I can ignore their accusations. There is nothing wrong with me." This is one way that your ego wants you to react to this: refusing to look at yourself. The other way that the ego wants to trap you is by submitting to the accusations of other people and letting your entire life revolve around avoiding these accusations.

One of the primary ways that people use a perversion of love, use love as a power game, is this threat that you are supposed to be a good person and that the worst thing, the worst sin, you could commit is to do something that causes others to accuse you of not being loving. Can you sense that your ego wants you to feel that if another person accuses you of not being loving, then that person must be right? There must be some reason why they are accusing you. It must mean that in some way you are not loving.

Can you not begin to see that it may very well be that they are projecting a false image upon you of what it means to be a loving person? You have no obligation to conform to that image, nor do you have an obligation to even respond to such accusations. You do not have to refute them. You do not have to accuse other people back whereby you engage in another power game. You do not have to explain it. You do not have to justify it.

What you need to do at this stage on your path is to engage in a process with me where *I* can show you at inner levels whether you are loving or not. You need to be open in your outer mind so that it can filter through to your conscious mind. You make the calls every night to go to my retreat while you are giving the invocations in this course. You open your mind to seeing something you have not seen before. You need to be open to the possibility that maybe you are not loving in certain ways.

Maybe you have some unresolved psychology. Maybe you have a habit pattern that is a power game. Maybe you are seeking to control other people through love. You also need to be open to the possibility that there are people around you who are doing that to you. At the same time, they are accusing you that you are doing it to them because they are projecting out their own unresolved psychology. You need to be open to both. You need to see through both so that you do not use the perversions of love as a power game against others, and you do not allow others to use them as a power game against you. Do you see? In order to pass the initiation, you need to overcome both the Alpha and the Omega.

You do not have to overcome this entirely on the first level of initiation at my retreat. Overcoming the power game of love is not just a matter of power. It has seven aspects. There is a perversion of each of the seven rays involved here, and that is why you will receive further instructions on the other rays at the other levels of initiation at my retreat.

Surrendering to the flow of Love

Fear not; despair not. Be willing to recognize that if this dictation has shocked you, then who was it that was shocked? Was it the Conscious You or was it the ego? I humbly suggest the latter, but please, don' take my word for it. Allow yourself to tune in so that you might experience what it is.

The ultimate outcome of the first level of initiation at my retreat is that you have a conscious experience of what you have seen at the etheric level of your mind. You consciously experience how it is the ego that reacts and how the Conscious You actually feels a sense of relief.

The Conscious You never resists the River of Life. The ego always resists. When the Conscious You is seeing life through the filter of the ego, it is still not resisting; it is just experiencing life through the filter of the ego's resistance. When you learn to tell the difference between those two, you have taken a very significant step forward on your path. Now you can begin to know that the ultimate power in the material world is the power of surrendering to the flow of love.

Paul the Venetian I AM. I AM an ascended master and the Chohan of the Third Ray of Divine Love.

5 | I INVOKE LOVE TO CONSUME POWER GAMES

In the name I AM THAT I AM, Jesus Christ, I call to my I AM Presence to flow through the I Will Be Presence that I AM and give this invocation with full power. I call to beloved Elohim Heros and Amora and Hercules and Amazonia, Archangel Chamuel and Charity and Michael and Faith, Paul the Venetian and Master MORE to help us transcend all tendency to use love as a hidden power game. Help us see and surrender all patterns that block our oneness with Paul the Venetian and with our I AM Presences, including …

[Make personal calls]

1. Paul the Venetian, you are the master

1. Paul the Venetian, I submit myself unconditionally to you as my teacher, my Master. Help us overcome the sense of discouragement and the tendency to take the path and the teachings for granted.

O Heros-Amora, in your love so pink,
I care not what others about me may think,
in oneness with you, I claim a new day,
an innocent child, I frolic and play.

O Heros-Amora, a new life begun,
I laugh at the devil, the serious one,
I bathe in your glorious Ruby-Pink Sun,
knowing my God allows life to be fun.

2. Paul the Venetian, help us see when our egos have used the path and the teachings to create a new equilibrium where the ego feels it is in control. Help us experience that the Conscious You is created out of the Creator's being, which is not standing still but is the ever-flowing stream of life.

O Heros-Amora, life is such a joy,
I see that the world is like a great toy,
whatever my mind into it projects,
the mirror of life exactly reflects.

O Heros-Amora, I reap what I sow,
yet this is Plan B for helping me grow,
for truly, Plan A is that I join the flow,
immersed in the Infinite Love you bestow.

3. Paul the Venetian, help us overcome identification with the ego and the need to be in control of our path. Help us come to your retreat without any preoccupied opinion about who we are, who you are and what the path of initiation should be like.

O Heros-Amora, conditions you burn,
I know I AM free to take a new turn,
Immersed in the stream of infinite Love,
I know that my Spirit came from Above.

O Heros-Amora, awakened I see,
in true love is no conditionality,
the devil is stuck in his duality,
but I AM set free by Love's reality.

4. Paul the Venetian, help us overcome the ego's tendency to take an outer teaching and use it to form a mental image of how you should teach us. I am willing to have you challenge my mental images of how the world works, how God is, how I am.

O Heros-Amora, I feel that at last,
I've risen above the trap of my past,
in true love I claim my freedom to grow,
forever I'm one with Love's Infinite Flow.

O Heros-Amora, conditions are ties,
forming a net of serpentine lies,
your love has no bounds, forever it flies,
raising all life into Ruby-Pink skies.

5. Paul the Venetian, helps us see that you cannot teach us how to transcend our mental images by conforming to or validating them. I want you to tell me what my ego and the false hierarchy do not want me to hear.

O Hercules Blue, you fill every space,
with infinite Power and infinite Grace,
you embody the key to creativity,
the will to transcend into Infinity.

O Hercules Blue, in oneness with thee,
I open my heart to your reality,
in feeling your flame, so clearly I see,
transcending my self is the true alchemy.

6. Paul the Venetian, help us transcend our graven images of the ascended masters. I am willing to shatter these mental images, and especially my image of love.

O Hercules Blue, I lovingly raise,
my voice in giving God infinite praise,
I'm grateful for playing my personal part,
In God's infinitely intricate work of art.

O Hercules Blue, all life now you heal,
enveloping all in your Blue-flame Seal,
your electric-blue fire within us reveal,
our innermost longing for all that is real.

7. Paul the Venetian, help us see the ego's tendency to use love in a power game aimed at controlling other people. I am willing to have you challenge my sense that I already know what love is, what it isn't, how it should be expressed and how it should not be expressed.

O Hercules Blue, I pledge now my life,
in helping this planet transcend human strife,
duality's lies are pierced by your light,
restoring the fullness of my inner sight.

O Hercules Blue, I'm one with your will,
all space in my being with Blue Flame you fill,
your power allows me to forge on until,
I pierce every veil and climb every hill.

8. Paul the Venetian, help us transcend our sense of what kind of initiations you should give us. Show us if we are seeking to use our images of love to overpower you. I accept that you are the teacher and I am the student.

> O Hercules Blue, your Temple of Light,
> revealed to us all through our inner sight,
> a beacon that radiates light to the earth,
> bringing about our planet's rebirth.
>
> **O Hercules Blue, all life you defend,**
> **giving us power to always transcend,**
> **in you the expansion of self has no end,**
> **as I in God's infinite spirals ascend.**

9. Paul the Venetian, help us transcend the misunderstood concept of love as a disguised power game. I accept that you cannot be moved, that you are immovable by any power game on earth, no matter how cleverly disguised as love.

> Accelerate into Oneness, I AM real,
> Accelerate into Oneness, all life heal,
> Accelerate into Oneness, I AM MORE,
> Accelerate into Oneness, all will soar.
>
> Accelerate into Oneness! (3X)
> Beloved Heros and Amora.
> Accelerate into Oneness! (3X)
> Beloved Chamuel and Charity.
> Accelerate into Oneness! (3X)
> Beloved Paul the Venetian.
> Accelerate into Oneness! (3X)
> Beloved I AM.

2. We are transcending our power games

1. Paul the Venetian, show us the perversions of love in our energy fields and how we have used them in our interactions with each other. Show us how we have used perverted love against others or have allowed others to use it against us.

Chamuel Archangel, in ruby ray power,
I know I am taking a life-giving shower.
Love burning away all perversions of will,
I suddenly feel my desires falling still.

Chamuel Archangel, descend from Above,
Chamuel Archangel, with ruby-pink love,
Chamuel Archangel, so often thought-of,
Chamuel Archangel, o come Holy Dove.

2. Paul the Venetian, show us if we have been overpowered or persuaded into accepting that a perversion of love was actually love. Help us overcome all tendency to think that the perversions of love are real love.

Chamuel Archangel, a spiral of light,
as ruby ray fire now pierces the night.
All forces of darkness consumed by your fire,
consuming all those who will not rise higher.

Chamuel Archangel, descend from Above,
Chamuel Archangel, with ruby-pink love,
Chamuel Archangel, so often thought-of,
Chamuel Archangel, o come Holy Dove.

3. Paul the Venetian, help us experience true love as the healer of the shock of seeing anti-love. I am willing give up my images of what I think is true love, what I have been conditioned to see as true love, what I have been programmed to accept as true love.

Chamuel Archangel, your love so immense,
with clarified vision, my life now makes sense.
The purpose of life you so clearly reveal,
immersed in your love, God's oneness I feel.

Chamuel Archangel, descend from Above,
Chamuel Archangel, with ruby-pink love,
Chamuel Archangel, so often thought-of,
Chamuel Archangel, o come Holy Dove.

4. Paul the Venetian, help us see through and rise above any power game we are engaged in with other people or each other. Help us be free of all desire to use perverted love against others and all desire to submit to such games from other people.

Chamuel Archangel, what calmness you bring,
I see now that even death has no sting.
For truly, in love there can be no decay,
as love is transcendence into a new day.

Chamuel Archangel, descend from Above,
Chamuel Archangel, with ruby-pink love,
Chamuel Archangel, so often thought-of,
Chamuel Archangel, o come Holy Dove.

5. Paul the Venetian, help us see the process of our outer minds questioning, arguing against, seeking to deny or refute the higher vision of love you are giving us. Help us see how our outer minds are playing a control game with us and how subtle the ego can be in using love.

Michael Archangel, in your flame so blue,
there is no more night, there is only you.
In oneness with you, I am filled with your light,
what glorious wonder, revealed to my sight.

Michael Archangel, your Faith is so strong,
Michael Archangel, oh sweep me along.
Michael Archangel, I'm singing your song,
Michael Archangel, with you I belong.

6. Paul the Venetian, help us overcome the ego's fear of loss. Help us experience that when we are in the flow of the energies of love there is no fear because love is always flowing.

Michael Archangel, protection you give,
within your blue shield, I ever shall live.
Sealed from all creatures, roaming the night,
I remain in your sphere, of electric blue light.

Michael Archangel, your Faith is so strong,
Michael Archangel, oh sweep me along.
Michael Archangel, I'm singing your song,
Michael Archangel, with you I belong.

7. Paul the Venetian, help us grasp that when we are always flowing with the River of Life there can be no real loss. Help us know that movement is the nature of the Conscious You and still-stand is the nature of the ego.

Michael Archangel, what power you bring,
as millions of angels, praises will sing.
Consuming the demons, of doubt and of fear,
I know that your Presence, will always be near.

Michael Archangel, your Faith is so strong,
Michael Archangel, oh sweep me along.
Michael Archangel, I'm singing your song,
Michael Archangel, with you I belong.

8. Paul the Venetian, help us see that it is the ego that has created the illusion that things can stand still and that a certain condition can be maintained over time. Help us see how this springs from the ego's desire for control through ownership.

Michael Archangel, God's will is your love,
you bring to us all, God's light from Above.
God's will is to see, all life taking flight,
transcendence of self, our most sacred right.

Michael Archangel, your Faith is so strong,
Michael Archangel, oh sweep me along.
Michael Archangel, I'm singing your song,
Michael Archangel, with you I belong.

9. Paul the Venetian, help us see how the ego thinks ownership is the key to control. Help us see that the perversion of love on the first ray of power is ownership, the very concept that we can own something on earth.

With angels I soar,
as I reach for MORE.
The angels so real,
their love all will heal.
The angels bring peace,
all conflicts will cease.
With angels of light,
we soar to new height.

The rustling sound of angel wings,
what joy as even matter sings,
what joy as every atom rings,
in harmony with angel wings.

3. We overcome the illusion of ownership

1. Paul the Venetian, help us see that in the ascended realm we own nothing because we have become one with the River of Life and there is no still-stand in the river. Help us overcome the desire to stand still.

Master Paul, venetian dream,
your love for beauty's flowing stream.
Master Paul, in love's own womb,
your power shatters ego's tomb.

O Holy Spirit, flow through me,
I am the open door for thee.
O mighty rushing stream of Light,
transcendence is my sacred right.

2. Paul the Venetian, show us how we subconsciously abuse love energy in any control game. I will not argue that you are wrong and I will not leave in a huff. I am willing to transcend the control games of my ego.

Master Paul, your counsel wise,
my mind is raised to lofty skies.
Master Paul, in wisdom's love,
such beauty flowing from Above.

O Holy Spirit, flow through me,
I am the open door for thee.
O mighty rushing stream of Light,
transcendence is my sacred right.

3. Paul the Venetian, help us grasp that what the ego sees is a reflection of what it is projecting into the mirror. Help us see that what our egos tell us is coming from the world or other people is actually a reflection of what we are sending out at subconscious levels.

Master Paul, love is an art,
it opens up the secret heart.
Master Paul, love's rushing flow,
my heart awash in sacred glow.

O Holy Spirit, flow through me,
I am the open door for thee.
O mighty rushing stream of Light,
transcendence is my sacred right.

4. Paul the Venetian, help us see that when we are using the perversions of love as a power game, we think we are being loving. Help us see that when we think other people are not loving, it is our egos that are not loving.

Master Paul, accelerate,
upon pure love I meditate.
Master Paul, intentions pure,
my self-transcendence will ensure.

O Holy Spirit, flow through me,
I am the open door for thee.
O mighty rushing stream of Light,
transcendence is my sacred right.

5. Paul the Venetian, help us see how our love relationships have been dominated or affected by the ego's tendency to create an appearance of being loving but it is not true love; it is a perversion of love.

Master Paul, your love will heal,
my inner light you do reveal.
Master Paul, all life console,
with you I'm being truly whole.

O Holy Spirit, flow through me,
I am the open door for thee.
O mighty rushing stream of Light,
transcendence is my sacred right.

6. Paul the Venetian, help us tune in to our Divine plans and assert our right to follow them regardless of what other people want from us. Help us see how our sense that we have a responsibility towards others is being used in a control game.

Master Paul, you serve the All,
by helping us transcend the fall.
Master Paul, in peace we rise,
as ego meets its sure demise.

O Holy Spirit, flow through me,
I am the open door for thee.
O mighty rushing stream of Light,
transcendence is my sacred right.

7. Paul the Venetian, help us fulfill both the Alpha and the Omega aspects of our responsibility. Help us respond when our I AM Presences release the matrix or a new phase of our Divine plans. Help us do the best we can to take care of our worldly situations, including other people.

Master Paul, love all life free,
your love is for eternity.
Master Paul, you are the One,
to help us make the journey fun.

O Holy Spirit, flow through me,
I am the open door for thee.
O mighty rushing stream of Light,
transcendence is my sacred right.

8. Paul the Venetian, help us transcend the satanic consciousness that demands Spirit should conform to matter. Help us transcend the illusion that in order to be responsible, our spirits must conform to the demands of the material world.

Master Paul, you balance all,
the seven rays upon my call.
Master Paul, you paint the sky,
with colors that delight the I.

O Holy Spirit, flow through me,
I am the open door for thee.
O mighty rushing stream of Light,
transcendence is my sacred right.

9. Paul the Venetian, help us set our priorities straight so we see that responding to Spirit is our primary responsibility. Responding to matter happens within the framework of Spirit, within the framework of our Divine plans. No one has the right to demand that we abort our Divine plans.

Master Paul, your Presence here,
filling up my inner sphere.
Life is now a sacred flow,
God Love I do on all bestow.

O Holy Spirit, flow through me,
I am the open door for thee.
O mighty rushing stream of Light,
transcendence is my sacred right.

4. We are truly response-able

1. Paul the Venetian, help us transcend the feeling that we have to submit to the demands of other people. Help us go beyond the sense that we are supposed to be loving and if we are really loving, we are supposed to be submissive and responsive to the needs, desires and demands of other people.

Master MORE, come to the fore,
I will absorb your flame of MORE.
Master MORE, my will so strong,
my power center cleared by song.

O Holy Spirit, flow through me,
I am the open door for thee.
O mighty rushing stream of Light,
transcendence is my sacred right.

2. Paul the Venetian, help us transcend the tendency to fear that other people accuse us of not being loving, not being kind, not being good persons, good children, good parents or good spouses.

Master MORE, your wisdom flows,
as my attunement ever grows.
Master MORE, we have a tie,
that helps me see through Serpent's lie.

O Holy Spirit, flow through me,
I am the open door for thee.
O mighty rushing stream of Light,
transcendence is my sacred right.

3. Paul the Venetian, help us see that the fear of being accused of not being loving comes from the ego playing a power game on us. It is trying to own us by making us think we have to submit to the worldly image of what it means to be a loving person.

Master MORE, your love so pink,
there is no purer love, I think.
Master MORE, you set me free,
from all conditionality.

O Holy Spirit, flow through me,
I am the open door for thee.
O mighty rushing stream of Light,
transcendence is my sacred right.

4. Paul the Venetian, help us transcend the image that our egos have created. I am willing to transcend this power game, even if it causes me to be accused of not being loving.

Master MORE, I will endure,
your discipline that makes me pure.
Master MORE, intentions true,
as I am always one with you.

O Holy Spirit, flow through me,
I am the open door for thee.
O mighty rushing stream of Light,
transcendence is my sacred right.

5. Paul the Venetian, help us see when our egos and other people are projecting a false image upon us of what it means to be a loving person. Help us accept that we have no obligation to conform to that image or respond to such accusations.

Master MORE, my vision raised,
the will of God is always praised.
Master MORE, creative will,
raising all life higher still.

O Holy Spirit, flow through me,
I am the open door for thee.
O mighty rushing stream of Light,
transcendence is my sacred right.

6. Paul the Venetian, show us at inner levels whether we are loving or not. I am willing to have this filter through my conscious mind. I am open to the possibility that maybe I am not loving in certain ways, that I have some unresolved psychology.

Master MORE, your peace is power,
the demons of war it will devour.
Master MORE, we serve all life,
our flames consuming war and strife.

O Holy Spirit, flow through me,
I am the open door for thee.
O mighty rushing stream of Light,
transcendence is my sacred right.

7. Paul the Venetian, help us see when people around us are projecting their unresolved psychology at us and then accusing us of doing to them what they are doing to us.

Master MORE, I am so free,
eternal bond from you to me.
Master MORE, I find rebirth,
in flow of your eternal mirth.

O Holy Spirit, flow through me,
I am the open door for thee.
O mighty rushing stream of Light,
transcendence is my sacred right.

8. Paul the Venetian, help us have a conscious experience of what we have seen at the etheric level of our minds. Help us consciously experience how the ego reacts and how the Conscious You never resists the River of Life.

Master MORE, you balance all,
the seven rays upon my call.
Master MORE, forever MORE,
I am the Spirit's open door.

O Holy Spirit, flow through me,
I am the open door for thee.
O mighty rushing stream of Light,
transcendence is my sacred right.

9. Paul the Venetian, help us see that the ego always resists and the Conscious You flows. Teach us how to tell the difference between the two so we can know that the ultimate power in the material world is the power of surrendering to the flow of love.

Master MORE, your Presence here,
filling up my inner sphere.
Life is now a sacred flow,
God Power I on all bestow.

O Holy Spirit, flow through me,
I am the open door for thee.
O mighty rushing stream of Light,
transcendence is my sacred right.

Sealing:

In the name of the Divine Mother, I fully accept that the power of these calls is used to set free the Ma-ter light, so it can outpicture the perfect vision of Christ for my own life, for all people and for the planet. In the name I AM THAT I AM, it is done! Amen.

6 | LOVE AND WISDOM

I AM Paul the Venetian. I come to discourse on what initiations you face on the second level of my retreat. Take note that I did not say that at the first level you have to completely overcome all tendency to use love as a power game. You might as well begin to realize that the human ego has a desire to come up with some ultimate thing. This is an expression of its desire for control. For example, it thinks that if it comes up with the ultimate theory, then it will be able to establish this ultimate control over its situation, its destiny or over the world, other people or God.

This is especially something that you need to deal with whenever you deal with the initiations of wisdom. My beloved brother, Lanto, has attempted to help you overcome this tendency on the Second Ray, but it is my task, my joy, to help you overcome it on the Third Ray. On the second level of initiation at my retreat, you face the task of dealing with love in connection with the Second Ray of Wisdom.

The patterns for current love relationships

This is when you need to begin to see the tendency, so prevalent in the world but especially in the Western world, of wanting to understand everything and of saying that if you understand something, it means understanding it intellectually. You may do well to read between the lines of what Lanto explained in his book about the limitations of the mind, the limitations of the intellect, but I would give you more concerning the intellect and love, especially love relationships.

We have entered a phase in the evolution of this planet and of humankind where the old patterns of love relationships are being challenged and often broken up. You will see, for example, that in many parts of the world, especially the so-called developed world, there are now more divorces than in recent, known history. There are various reasons for this, but the underlying reason is precisely that in order to enter the Aquarian Age, you cannot carry on the patterns of relationships seen not only in Pisces but even in ages before Pisces.

The polarities of masculine and feminine

The relationships between men and women on this planet have been locked in an imbalanced track for a very long time. You can see in your own tradition, the so-called Judeo-Christian tradition, how, even going back to Old Testament times, the relationship between men and women was locked in a certain pattern that defines women as inherently inferior to men.

Look at the creation story in the Old Testament. First, God creates man, and then, as a kind of afterthought, God creates women as a support or a help for men. Do you really think that this is how creation took place? If you do, then I can assure you that when you come to the second level at my retreat, you will find cause to challenge that perception.

What have we of the ascended masters now expressed for a long time through this messenger? We have expressed that there is one undivided, indivisible Creator, but that, when the Creator decided to create, the first act of creation was a polarity between two forces: The expanding and the contracting, which can be translated to masculine and feminine. Do you really think that you can create a polarity by first creating one aspect of the polarity and then creating the other? Do you really think that in a polarity one aspect is superior to the other? In a polarity, both are created at the same time, and they are created in a symbiotic relationship so that they balance each other.

I said in my first discourse that Spirit is primary on earth in the sense that you need to follow your Divine plan more than the demands of the world. You cannot let your Spirit conform to the demands of the world. This is so because the earth is in an unascended sphere where there is much imbalance. How can you help your sphere ascend? You do not help your sphere ascend by conforming to the conditions that spring from the unascended state of consciousness, the consciousness of separation.

That is why Spirit must be primary, and that is the basis for the Biblical statement that the husband is the master of the household. This is symbolic only. It was never meant to mean that the man is superior to the woman. It was never meant to mean that the masculine aspect of the Divine polarity is somehow superior to the feminine, that the feminine was the one who caused the fall and that this should now be blamed on women on earth. It did not mean that women should be put down in some inferior relationship of serving men and obeying and keeping their mouth shut in the churches.

Balancing the feminine polarity

This entire consciousness of putting down women has come from the fallen beings. They saw an opportunity to create such a deep imbalance between the two sexes that they could never come together in a relationship of equals where the man and the woman in a relationship could outpicture the fullness of the

Divine polarity. The fallen beings have set a pattern that makes it very difficult, almost impossible, to have a physical love relationship in the material octave that fulfills its highest creative potential. This is what needs to be overcome in the golden age.

When you are at this particular level at my retreat, you do not have to completely overcome this tendency all at once, but you do need to become aware of it. You need to recognize that if you are in a relationship with a person of the opposite sex, there is a need for both of you to work on transcending this false polarity, the unbalanced relationship where the female is so often seen as somehow inferior to the male.

I know that many of you will say that you have grown up in the modern age. You often feel that your parents were locked in the old kind of relationship with a certain role defined for women. You have been more modern, you have been more balanced. I do not dispute that you have been more balanced than your parents. Most of you certainly have. What I am saying is that there is still more to overcome concerning the relationship between the two sexes.

Divine love cannot be owned

Love is the great equalizer. Love cannot be owned. This is what you might have taken from my first discourse, if you have read between the lines. Most people think that the ego's power game of ownership and control is about owning or controlling something in the physical octave.

The ego is also about owning and controlling certain creative qualities so that the ego can pervert them and shut them out of this world. The ego wants to pervert your view of love so that you cannot be an open door for Divine love to flow through you. This Divine love can consume the imbalances in all relationships on earth, but only if it is allowed to flow freely. If you pervert it, if you seek to direct it into a certain thought matrix based on the consciousness of separation, love cannot flow freely. Then it cannot heal with the maximum effect. How can love heal you when you are seeking to make it conform to the very image that causes you to need healing? It is an unbalanced image that causes you to need the healing in the first place. If you seek to force love to flow according to the unbalanced image, then you will not have Divine love. Whatever flows through you will not have the maximum healing power.

Is this not logical? Is the intellect not proud of being able to use logic? What you need to accomplish, as the Conscious You, is to learn how to use logic against the intellectual, analytical, rational mind. I do not mean "against" in the sense that you are engaging in a battle with your own mind. You use logic to avoid being pulled into the patterns created by this mind.

Overcoming the imbalance between the sexes

What do you see in the modern world in the relationship between men and women? On the outer, you see that more marriages end in divorce than ever before. Behind that, you see a shift in the dynamic between the sexes. This shift has many facets, but it is really driven by the need to overcome thousands of years of imbalance. It is not just men who have created or upheld this imbalance. Do not be fooled into thinking that it was the men in physical embodiment who created the imbalance in the first place and who are primarily responsible for maintaining it.

You are dealing with forces beyond the physical who created the imbalance and who are managing to maintain it through those in physical embodiment who are willing instruments. What needs to happen is that you no longer be a willing instrument because you rise above this dynamic. You need to realize that the dynamic between men and women is not something you can blame on the men.

What is the dynamic that has been going on ever since the Old Testament story of the fall in the Garden of Eden? It is that men have been blaming women for the fall. Do you think that you make progress by creating a culture where women are now blaming men for the suppression of women? How can you overcome blame by adding more blame? Men did not start this cycle. They became the victims of it, as women became the victims of it. You also need to realize that women have willingly, although rarely *knowingly*, submitted to this.

They have taken up their role for thousands of years. The women on this planet have accepted themselves as being inferior based on the physical differences between male and female bodies. They have also accepted themselves as inferior based on some philosophical overlay, often promoted by this, that or the next religion. Even in the East, where you have religions that are not based on the Old Testament, you still see an inequality among the sexes. You still see that women are put down or considered virtually useless because daughters cannot easily be married away.

Blame as a perversion of love

You cannot blame this on the men. You cannot blame this exclusively on the Judeo-Christian tradition. You could blame it on the fallen beings, but that is not really constructive. The problem with the consciousness is that it uses another perversion of love, the primary one being fear, but blame being one of the secondary perversions. What you need to do is to overcome the tendency, the need, to blame. You do this, if you are willing, at the second level of my retreat where you become aware that blame is a perversion of love.

What do you see in the modern world? You see an incredible expansion of knowledge, the knowledge of how everything works. Much of this knowledge has been achieved through the linear, analytical, intellectual mind. This mind has certain positive qualities. Do not be fooled into thinking that the intellectual mind is necessarily an enemy of your spiritual growth. It is only an enemy when it is used in an unbalanced way, which is exactly what your ego and the fallen beings want. You can rise above this because the intellect is able to argue for or against any condition. The intellect is very good at creating an imbalanced view of life, but you can use the logic of the intellect to make this contradiction, this imbalance, visible. Then the Conscious You can step out of it. Instead of identifying itself with the intellect and the intellect's view of life, you can see the intellect as merely a tool for accomplishing certain tasks in the physical octave.

You can stop using the intellect to reason about that which is beyond the physical octave because you can recognize a truth known by all mystics throughout the ages. This truth is that the intellect can never give you accurate understanding of the higher world. The Buddha recognized this 2,500 years ago, which is why he didn't give a teaching about the heaven world but gave a teaching about how to take control over your own mind. You would raise your consciousness until you could experience the higher world directly in a way that is beyond the understanding and the analysis of the intellect.

In the modern world there has been an increased awareness, but as the old saying goes: "If the only tool you have is a hammer, you think every problem is a nail." If the only tool you have is the intellect, you think every problem must be solved by analyzing it. Do you see what has happened between men and women? There has been an increase in the awareness around relationships. This is, in many ways, very good and very necessary.

It is necessary to break up the old, unbalanced dynamic between men and women. This can happen only through a raising of awareness, but it cannot happen only through intellectual knowledge. What you see in the modern Western world is that men and women have attempted to analyze their way out of relationship problems. It is an underlying force, the force of growth, that has caused there to be more problems in relationships.

The difficulty in maintaining unbalanced relationships

An unbalanced relationship is difficult to maintain, much more difficult today than it was in your parents' generation. Most of you can go back and see that in your parents' generation, they were able to stay married for forty or fifty years. This was partly because they found some mutual imbalanced state of balance where they could live with each other without challenging each other. While this gave a certain outer harmony, it did not create growth.

This state of unbalanced equilibrium is more difficult to maintain today, and that is why many of you have had problems in your relationships. It is more difficult to maintain a relationship that is not growing. There will be an inner sense that one or both partners are not satisfied, that something isn't right, that the relationship isn't living up to its highest potential, that something needs to change.

What do many of you do then? You either read a book or you go to a counselor, and you look for some intellectual understanding of what is wrong with your relationship so that you can attempt to fix it. This is both the strength and the curse of the Western world: the tendency to analyze everything. You think that by reducing everything to its basic components, you can understand the cause. When you change the cause, you will also change the effects. You think that if there is a problem between men and women in relationships, you need to break down everything into its components.

Say you have a relationship between a man and a woman. You now focus on the man and you focus on the woman. You say: "What is the characteristic of men? What is the characteristic of women?" You come up with a wonderful sounding theory that "men are from Mars and women are from Venus." Then you analyze certain characteristics of men and you say: "Men do this, and it has that effect on women. Women do this, and it has that effect on men. If men learn to know what they are doing and how it affects the women, then they can change so that they don't produce the negative effect in women. If women learn about themselves, then they can also change, and then they can live happily ever after."

My beloved, it is very important here that you step up and go beyond what the intellect always wants to do, namely to reduce everything to its basic components. It wants to believe that now it has found the bottom line, the deepest cause. When it understands things at that level, it will understand everything it needs to understand at the other levels as well.

What have physicists been trying to do in understanding the physical world? They first look at the surface appearances. Then they see that everything is made out of matter. Matter is made out of molecules. Molecules are made out of atoms. Atoms are made out of subatomic particles. The intellectual materialists say: "By finding subatomic particles, we have reduced the world to its basic components. Now it is just a matter of understanding how these subatomic particles work and finding the ultimate particle, the god-particle. Then we will understand how the entire universe works." But, it is not so.

Using intuition to go beyond the intellect

The intellect has a fundamental limitation. By analyzing, by reducing something to its basic components, it loses what? It loses the whole. You may have heard the saying: "The whole is more than the sum of its parts." A relationship between a man and a woman is a whole. It is more than the sum of the man and the woman and the psychology of the man and the psychology of the woman and the biology of the man and the biology of the woman. It is more than that.

Now make the distinction that I want you to make. I am *not* saying that analyzing relationships or analyzing the psychology of men and women is wrong or that you should not do this. The modern world has made progress because it has analyzed and attempted to understand everything. What I am seeking to point out to you is that the progress of the modern world has also hit up against the outer limits of what can be achieved by analyzing, by reducing. What is needed in the Aquarian age – and what is essential for the Aquarian age becoming a golden age – is that people learn to take analysis as far as it can be taken and then use intuition to go beyond.

Some have always understood this. Einstein, for example, had some understanding of this and was able to make some intuitive breakthroughs. He was also unable to fully grasp what I have said here, which means that he did allow his intellect to impose a certain limitation on his intuitive abilities. That is why he could never finish his work and come up with the theory he so longed to find.

This was partly because he did not realize that his dream of an ultimate theory was the dream of the intellect and not the dream of the intuitive mind. It has no need for something that is ultimate in the physical, for it flows with the Spirit. It knows that the ultimate force, the ultimate reality, is flow.

Breaking the reactionary patterns in relationships

Nothing stands still so how can anything be ultimate—any "thing?" God is ultimate, but even God is not standing still. God is constantly transcending itself through you. Why would you, when you are God's self-transcending aspect, think that you can stand still? It is not logical. The fallen beings cannot see this, your ego cannot see this and your intellect cannot see this. You *can,* when you are conscious of yourself as unbound awareness. How does this relate to the relationship between men and women? Can you really reduce a man to a certain set of characteristics? You cannot!

What you *can* do is to help a man and a woman see: "My outer self has been trapped in a certain pattern. When my partner does or says certain things, my outer self reacts in a certain way and that means I say something back." You can also come to understand that when you react and say something to your partner, then your partner has another pattern that causes your partner to react a certain way. That means both of you go into a spiral that is created by the combination of your limiting patterns. You become trapped in this downward spiral where you pull each other down energetically.

This you can come to understand, and it is valuable for helping you break up these patterns—if you are willing to break them up, if *both* are willing to break them up. If only one partner is *not* willing to break up the pattern, then the relationship cannot necessarily transcend that level.

Receiving love, the antidote to fear

When all is said and done, you will not have a successful relationship only by analyzing yourselves and each other. You will have it only by realizing that love must always be flowing.

What is it that really causes relationships to be locked in these limiting patterns? It is the ego's fear of loss, which causes the ego to want to control your partner so that you cannot lose that which you think you can get only through your partner. All human beings on earth are somewhat affected by the consciousness of separation. If you were not, you would not be able to stay in embodiment. The lower you go towards the lowest level of consciousness, the more people are affected. The more you are affected by the consciousness of separation, the more you feel alone. You feel trapped in a threatening environment and your relationship to your environment is based on fear.

There is an inner knowing in all people that love is the antidote to fear. Many people are not aware of this consciously, but it is still there at a deeper level. This means that the more you become trapped in fear, the more you long for love.

How are you going to get love? As a child, you may be fortunate to get love from your parents, or at least one of your parents. Many children grow up with parents who are trapped below the 48th level of consciousness. When you are below the 48th level of consciousness, you are not able to give love freely. Your children will not feel they are getting enough love from you as a parent.

The other side of the equation is that if the child is below the 48th level, it will not be able to receive love freely. No matter how much love the parent gives, the child still would not feel it is enough. The basic dynamic is that most people grow up with a sense that they have not received enough love so they feel a deficit. They now go into the teenage years and their hormones kick in and they begin to have sexual feelings. Based on the common culture, they think that the way to get the love they long for is by finding a partner of the opposite sex and having a physical, romantic, sexual relationship.

The deficit of love

The vast majority of relationships on this planet start from a situation where both partners feel a deficit of love. Both partners think the relationship is meant to fill their love deficit. How will it do so? It will do so by you getting enough love from your partner. Your partner also has a deficit of love and feels that he or she has not received enough love growing up. I understand that you have grown up in a dysfunctional culture. You have grown up with a dysfunctional view of relationships. You have grown up with the expectation that your partner should be able to fill your need for love. I understand that you have this expectation. I am not blaming you for it. I am only asking you to consider whether it is *realistic*. Is it even *possible* that your partner could fill your need for love?

Your partner has grown up in the same culture as yourself. Your partner also has a deficit, a feeling that he or she has not received enough love. If *you* have a deficit, if *your partner* has a deficit, how is your partner going to be able to give you the love that you need if the partner does not have enough love in his or her energy field and chakras?

How will your partner have enough love to give you so that this can fill your needs? How can two people who both have a deficit help each other overcome the deficit? Does this make sense? Cannot even the intellect see that this is not a realistic expectation? If you start a relationship where both people have an unrealistic expectation of what the relationship is going to do, then there can only be one possible outcome: Both partners will be disappointed with the relationship.

Now you reason, as your culture has taught you to do, that this means there must be something wrong with the relationship: "I am not getting my need for love fulfilled by my partner. There must be something wrong. Since I am not getting what I need from my partner, there must be something wrong with my partner." Now, the two people go into a phase where, after having ignored the fact that they are both dissatisfied with the relationship, they begin to acknowledge and openly voice their dissatisfaction with the relationship.

They come to a point where they decide: "We have to do something." What do they do? They find a book, they listen to a course, they go to a counselor. They start having these exhausting conversations: "You did this! You didn't do this! You make me feel this way. You make me feel that way."

What are you trying to do here? If you are trying to become aware of your own dysfunctional patterns so that you can change those patterns, then you may have a chance of having benefit from this. If both partners are doing the same, and if both partners are willing to look at themselves and change their patterns, you can make progress this way. What too often happens is that both partners go into what I, in my first discourse, called the power game disguised as love. You are using the intellect to try to analyze your partner, and the purpose is to get your partner to change so that *you* do not have to change.

Solving the deficit through a focus on the whole

My beloved, this is the basic game of your ego: Never looking at the beam in your own eye, always looking at the splinter in the eye of your partner, always projecting that the problem is out there and that the solution must be that your partner changes while you do not have to. Or you may feel that if you have to change, then you cannot change until your partner has changed. If only your partner would change so that your partner would give you the love you need, then *you* would automatically change. How many of you have been in this situation? All of you have, this messenger certainly no exception. Can you not step up and see that this is just another example of a power game where you are using love as an excuse?

At the surface level, you may feel and honestly believe that you are only doing this because you want the relationship to work. You are only seeking to help your partner change so that he or she can snap out of these dysfunctional patterns. You may even feel that you are seeking to change yourself, to snap out of your patterns. Again, take note here. You *can* make progress by analyzing a relationship, the dynamic between you and your partner, and analyzing the psychology of you and your partner. You can make progress by doing this, but you will not make the maximum progress and you will not save the relationship by focusing on the reductionist, analytical process. You will not save the relationship by focusing on the lacks of yourself and your partner. A successful relationship, where there is maximum creativity, can be based on only one thing: a focus on the whole.

What is it you do when you analyze your partner? You are seeking to reduce your partner to a few characteristics, a few patterns in the psyche. You may have a good counselor who can point out some of the patterns that your partner and yourself have in the psyche, but what are you doing? The patterns are in the outer mind. The patterns are not in the Conscious You because the Conscious You is pure, undifferentiated awareness and does not have patterns. By reducing your partner or yourself to these patterns in the outer mind, what happens? You see only the trees, and you don't see the forest of the Conscious You that is the open door, the doorway, for the I AM Presence of your partner and yourself.

Your ego and the ego of your partner will never get along. Your outer mind and the outer mind of your partner will never truly be creative together. Your outer minds may be able to find a balance where there is not a constant conflict. Your two egos may go into this state of equilibrium where one has established superiority and the other has accepted inferiority. This may give you a balance of power where you can live together without constantly fighting.

Many people in the world call this a successful, even a harmonious, relationship. It is not a creative relationship because a creative relationship can only happen when both partners are seeking to become open doors for their I AM Presences. Becoming open doors means you overcome the patterns in your psychology so that you can be the Conscious You without any coloring from the outer mind—and you seek to help your partner do the same. The more you analyze your partner, the more you hold on to the idea: "Oh, he is this way" or "He is that way" or "She is like this" or "She always reacts like that." The more you do this, the more you obscure the Conscious You and its freedom to flow. The more you analyze, the less creative you will be. Again, there can be a benefit to analyzing in order to overcome patterns, but once you overcome the patterns, you need to take the next step up and allow each other to be.

Receiving love from your I AM Presence

Compare this to what I have said about the deficit of love, the need to have love, and the need to get it from your partner. You can do this only when both of you recognize that the purpose of a relationship between a man and a woman is *not* to give both partners love. The purpose is to be creative and bring forth something that is more than each of you could bring forth alone because the whole is allowed to become more than the sum of the parts.

You also need to recognize that, although you have a need for love, you will never receive enough love from your partner or any other human being. You cannot receive enough love from *outside* yourself. You can receive it only from *inside* yourself, from your I AM Presence. No partner on earth can love you like your I AM Presence does.

Many spiritual people have begun to rise above the worldly form of love, but they are still thinking that if their partner is really spiritual, he or she should be able to give them the love they need. I am not saying that your partner should not give you love when you live together in a love relationship. Surely, you express love towards each other, but if the relationship is going to be successful, you both need to overcome your deficit of love. You do not expect or demand that your partner should give you the love that you can receive only from your I AM Presence. There *is* love you can receive from your partner, but the love that you really need in order to overcome separation can only come from your I AM Presence.

It is *your* sole responsibility to establish a connection with your I AM Presence. This is not the responsibility of your partner. It is not even the responsibility of your guru, whether you see your guru as someone in embodiment or an ascended master. It is *your* responsibility.

You need to turn it into a "response-ability." You do what I said in my first discourse and establish the right priority. You realize that the love you long for, the love you really need, can *only* come from your I AM Presence, not from your partner. You do not expect or demand from your partner what you cannot get from your partner. You do not blame your partner for not giving you what you could not receive, even if your partner was able to give it.

Do you not understand? It is not just that your partner cannot *give* you the love you need. It is also that you cannot *receive* that love from any external source. You can only receive it from your I AM Presence.

Stop blaming your partner

What happens when you meet a partner and you fall in love? You go through this euphoric state where you feel the relationship is working and the love is flowing and you are finally getting, you think, the love you need. As most of you have realized, being in love is a state of illusion. It is a state of euphoria. It is a kind of drug.

When you are in love, you are setting aside some of your normal patterns. You are now able to receive a certain love from your I AM Presence. You just do not realize it is coming from your I AM Presence, and you think it is coming from your partner. What happens over time, why does the love fade away? Because your I AM Presence knows what you need to learn.

You need to establish a conscious awareness of the fact that the love you need can only come from your I AM Presence so that you begin to focus on your I AM Presence. Most people don't do this in a love relationship because you have no teaching that this is what you need. Then your I AM Presence must cut off the flow of love. It must cut it off, not as a punishment but as the only way for you to start thinking about why you are not getting the love you need.

Because of what they have been brought up to know in the world, most people go into a pattern of blaming their partner instead of focusing on establishing a conscious connection to the I AM Presence. I fully understand this. I have nothing but compassion and empathy for the many people who cannot *do* better because they do not *know* better.

What can I do about it, except give you the knowledge so that you *do* know better? I hope that those of you who are open to these teachings, and do know better, will do better for yourselves. I also hope you will spread the word to others that there is a different approach to relationships.

Balance between Alpha and Omega

Your ultimate fulfillment does not come from establishing this otherworldly love relationship to the perfect partner here on earth. Your ultimate fulfillment can come only by you establishing a relationship with your I AM Presence. You realize that your I AM Presence is the Alpha, the masculine aspect of your being. The Conscious You is the Omega, the feminine aspect of your being. Then you allow the I AM Presence to be the master of your household, and you accept that you are the Omega polarity in the material world to the Alpha polarity of your I AM Presence in the spiritual realm. There can now be the correct figure-eight flow in your own being (the vertical, figure-eight flow), and then you may establish the most creative figure-eight flow with your love partner here on earth. You can never establish the horizontal figure-eight flow before each of the partners has a high degree of the vertical figure-eight flow.

What does it mean that a man and a woman are complete equals? It can only be achieved when both recognize their relationship with the I AM Presence. They recognize and experience that the I AM Presence is in the spiritual realm and is beyond any value judgments or comparisons on earth. It is not a matter of being better than others. It is not a matter of one partner being superior to the other or being more important than the other.

Each of you has an I AM Presence that is a unique spiritual being. Each of you has a Divine plan. You are both equally important, and the relationship will find its most successful expression only if you allow both of you to fulfill your Divine plan.

I understand that sometimes you can, through this level of awareness, come to the realization that your Divine plans require such different outer circumstances and actions that it is not constructive or practical to maintain a love relationship. This is also a successful relationship.

A successful relationship is not one where the partners stay together for life; it is one where the two partners help each other on their individual journeys until they come to a point where they are ready to take the next step. If the two partners recognize that the next step on their journeys can best be accomplished by them not living together in a relationship, then this is also a success.

Marriage for life?

Where did the idea that a marriage should be kept together for life come from? It came in part from past ages where there was greater insecurity, and especially in societies where women had virtually no way of providing for themselves, where it was only the man who had a job or an occupation. As a practical, social tool, it was better that a man did not abandon his wife when she became a little older and could no longer fill his sexual desires. From a purely practical standpoint, there was a culture established that the man should stay with his wife.

This is valid in societies where the woman still has no way of making a living. Of course, such societies have long ago outlived their purpose. In a golden age, all societies on earth need to move to a state where both men and women can provide for themselves. As long as this is not achieved, then you cannot have a culture where a man can just leave a woman anytime he wants. On the other hand, in the modern industrialized world, where you have to a large degree moved beyond this dynamic, you need to recognize that the idea that a man and woman should stay together only comes from the fallen beings and the ego, which want to lock you at a certain level and stop your growth.

If a man and a woman can grow together in their relationship for an entire lifetime, then they should stay together. If they come to the realization that the growth of each of them requires that they flow in different directions, then they should flow in those different directions. Instead of blaming each other or feeling bad about this, they should be able to separate with a positive feeling and a sense of gratitude that they have helped each other reach this level.

If you cannot, then you are trapped in another power game. You are still trapped in the game of wanting to blame your partner, and that means you have not passed the initiation at the second level of my retreat. I will, of course, help you pass this initiation in my next discourse, which talks about the double dose of love that you get at the third level of my retreat.

I AM, Paul the Venetian.

7 | I INVOKE LOVE TO BALANCE THE INTELLECT

In the name I AM THAT I AM, Jesus Christ, I call to my I AM Presence to flow through the I Will Be Presence that I AM and give this invocation with full power. I call to beloved Elohim Heros and Amora and Apollo and Lumina, Archangel Chamuel and Charity and Jophiel and Christine, Paul the Venetian and Master Lanto to help us overcome all tendency to over-analyze and blame each other. Help us see and surrender all patterns that block our oneness with Paul the Venetian and with our I AM Presences, including …

[Make personal calls]

I. We know the relationship pattern for Aquarius

1. Paul the Venetian, help us overcome the ego's illusion that if it comes up with the ultimate theory, it will be able to establish full control over our situation, other people or God.

O Heros-Amora, in your love so pink,
I care not what others about me may think,
in oneness with you, I claim a new day,
an innocent child, I frolic and play.

O Heros-Amora, a new life begun,
I laugh at the devil, the serious one,
I bathe in your glorious Ruby-Pink Sun,
knowing my God allows life to be fun.

2. Paul the Venetian, help us overcome the tendency of wanting to understand everything, thinking that understanding something means understanding it intellectually.

O Heros-Amora, life is such a joy,
I see that the world is like a great toy,
whatever my mind into it projects,
the mirror of life exactly reflects.

O Heros-Amora, I reap what I sow,
yet this is Plan B for helping me grow,
for truly, Plan A is that I join the flow,
immersed in the Infinite Love you bestow.

3. Paul the Venetian, help us transcend the patterns for love relationships established in the Age of Pisces. Help us discover the relationship patterns suitable for Aquarius.

O Heros-Amora, conditions you burn,
I know I AM free to take a new turn,
Immersed in the stream of infinite Love,
I know that my Spirit came from Above.

O Heros-Amora, awakened I see,
in true love is no conditionality,
the devil is stuck in his duality,
but I AM set free by Love's reality.

4. Paul the Venetian, help us transcend the pattern that defines women as inherently inferior to men. Help us accept that men and women are created as equals in a symbiotic relationship so we can balance each other.

O Heros-Amora, I feel that at last,
I've risen above the trap of my past,
in true love I claim my freedom to grow,
forever I'm one with Love's Infinite Flow.

O Heros-Amora, conditions are ties,
forming a net of serpentine lies,
your love has no bounds, forever it flies,
raising all life into Ruby-Pink skies.

5. Paul the Venetian, help us grasp that Spirit is the "head of the household" in the psyche of both men and women. The I AM Presence is the masculine polarity and the Conscious You is the feminine polarity.

Beloved Apollo, with your second ray,
you open my eyes to see a new day,
I see through duality's lies and deceit,
transcending the mindset producing defeat.

Beloved Apollo, thou Elohim Gold,
your radiant light my eyes now behold,
as pages of wisdom you gently unfold,
I feel I am free from all that is old.

6. Paul the Venetian, help us transcend the consciousness of putting down women. Help us rise above the plot of the fallen beings that makes it difficult to have a love relationship that fulfills its highest creative potential.

Beloved Apollo, in your flame I know,
that your living wisdom is always a flow,
in your light I see my own highest will,
immersed in the stream that never stands still.

Beloved Apollo, your light makes it clear,
why we have taken embodiment here,
working to raise our own cosmic sphere,
together we form the tip of the spear.

7. Paul the Venetian, help us grasp that love is the great equalizer. Help us overcome the ego's subtle power games so we can be the open doors for Divine love to flow through us.

Beloved Apollo, exposing all lies,
I hereby surrender all ego-based ties,
I know my perception is truly the key,
to transcending the serpentine duality.

Beloved Apollo, we heed now your call,
drawing us into Wisdom's Great Hall,
exposing all lies causing the fall,
you help us reclaim the oneness of all.

8. Paul the Venetian, help us see any tendency to pervert love through the consciousness of separation. Help us be open doors so Divine love can flow freely through us and heal with the maximum effect.

Beloved Apollo, your wisdom so clear,
in oneness with you, no serpent I fear,
the beam in my eye I'm willing to see,
I'm free from the serpent's own duality.

Beloved Apollo, my eyes now I raise,
I see that the earth is in a new phase,
I willingly stand in your piercing gaze,
empowered, I exit duality's maze.

9. Paul the Venetian, help us learn how to use logic to balance the intellectual, analytical, rational mind so we can avoid being pulled into the rigid patterns created by this mind.

Accelerate into Oneness, I AM real,
Accelerate into Oneness, all life heal,
Accelerate into Oneness, I AM MORE,
Accelerate into Oneness, all will soar.

Accelerate into Oneness! (3X)
Beloved Heros and Amora.
Accelerate into Oneness! (3X)
Beloved Chamuel and Charity.
Accelerate into Oneness! (3X)
Beloved Paul the Venetian.
Accelerate into Oneness! (3X)
Beloved I AM.

2. We are rising above all tendency to blame

1. Paul the Venetian, help us grasp that one cannot overcome blame by adding more blame because blame is a perversion of love. Help us transcend the age-old patterns of men and women blaming each other.

Chamuel Archangel, in ruby ray power,
I know I am taking a life-giving shower.
Love burning away all perversions of will,
I suddenly feel my desires falling still.

Chamuel Archangel, descend from Above,
Chamuel Archangel, with ruby-pink love,
Chamuel Archangel, so often thought-of,
Chamuel Archangel, o come Holy Dove.

2. Paul the Venetian, help us rise above the age-old pattern of women accepting themselves as being inferior based on some philosophical overlay promoted by religion.

Chamuel Archangel, a spiral of light,
as ruby ray fire now pierces the night.
All forces of darkness consumed by your fire,
consuming all those who will not rise higher.

Chamuel Archangel, descend from Above,
Chamuel Archangel, with ruby-pink love,
Chamuel Archangel, so often thought-of,
Chamuel Archangel, o come Holy Dove.

3. Paul the Venetian, help us overcome the tendency of men and women attempting to analyze their way out of relationship problems.

Chamuel Archangel, your love so immense,
with clarified vision, my life now makes sense.
The purpose of life you so clearly reveal,
immersed in your love, God's oneness I feel.

Chamuel Archangel, descend from Above,
Chamuel Archangel, with ruby-pink love,
Chamuel Archangel, so often thought-of,
Chamuel Archangel, o come Holy Dove.

4. Paul the Venetian, help us grasp why it is now more difficult to maintain a relationship that isn't growing. Help us see that the way out is not to reduce everything to its basic components.

Chamuel Archangel, what calmness you bring,
I see now that even death has no sting.
For truly, in love there can be no decay,
as love is transcendence into a new day.

Chamuel Archangel, descend from Above,
Chamuel Archangel, with ruby-pink love,
Chamuel Archangel, so often thought-of,
Chamuel Archangel, o come Holy Dove.

5. Paul the Venetian, help us grasp that the whole is more than the sum of its parts. A relationship between a man and a woman is a whole and it is more than the sum of the psychology and biology of the man and the woman.

Jophiel Archangel, in wisdom's great light,
all serpentine lies exposed to my sight.
So subtle the lies that creep through the mind,
yet you are the greatest teacher I find.

Jophiel Archangel, exposing all lies,
Jophiel Archangel, cutting all ties.
Jophiel Archangel, clearing the skies,
Jophiel Archangel, my mind truly flies.

6. Paul the Venetian, help us see the need to increase our understanding of relationships and at the same time learn to take analysis as far as it can be taken and then use intuition to go beyond.

Jophiel Archangel, your wisdom I hail,
your sword cutting through duality's veil.
As you show the way, I know what is real,
from serpentine doubt, I instantly heal.

Jophiel Archangel, exposing all lies,
Jophiel Archangel, cutting all ties.
Jophiel Archangel, clearing the skies,
Jophiel Archangel, my mind truly flies.

7. Paul the Venetian, help us see how our outer selves have been trapped in certain patterns that cause us to react to each other.

Jophiel Archangel, your reality,
the best antidote to duality.
No lie can remain in your Presence so clear,
with you on my side, no serpent I fear.

Jophiel Archangel, exposing all lies,
Jophiel Archangel, cutting all ties.
Jophiel Archangel, clearing the skies,
Jophiel Archangel, my mind truly flies.

8. Paul the Venetian, help us see how the combination of our limiting patterns have trapped us in a downward spiral where we pull each other down energetically.

Jophiel Archangel, God's mind is in me,
and through your clear light, its wisdom I see.
Divisions all vanish, as I see the One,
and truly, the wholeness of mind I have won.

Jophiel Archangel, exposing all lies,
Jophiel Archangel, cutting all ties.
Jophiel Archangel, clearing the skies,
Jophiel Archangel, my mind truly flies.

9. Paul the Venetian, help us see that love must always be flowing. We must transcend the ego's fear of loss and the desire to control one's partner so that one cannot lose that which the ego thinks it can get only through the partner.

With angels I soar,
as I reach for MORE.
The angels so real,
their love all will heal.
The angels bring peace,
all conflicts will cease.
With angels of light,
we soar to new height.

The rustling sound of angel wings,
what joy as even matter sings,
what joy as every atom rings,
in harmony with angel wings.

3. We transcend unrealistic expectations

1. Paul the Venetian, help us see any tendency to think that we need love from a partner in order to overcome our own internal fear. Help us see how to deal with the fear directly inside ourselves.

Master Paul, venetian dream,
your love for beauty's flowing stream.
Master Paul, in love's own womb,
your power shatters ego's tomb.

O Holy Spirit, flow through me,
I am the open door for thee.
O mighty rushing stream of Light,
transcendence is my sacred right.

2. Paul the Venetian, help us overcome any deficit of love from our upbringing so that we do not demand that a partner should fill our love deficit, the deficit that can only be filled by resolving the psychology that causes us to reject love from the I AM Presence.

Master Paul, your counsel wise,
my mind is raised to lofty skies.
Master Paul, in wisdom's love,
such beauty flowing from Above.

O Holy Spirit, flow through me,
I am the open door for thee.
O mighty rushing stream of Light,
transcendence is my sacred right.

3. Paul the Venetian, help us transcend the unrealistic expectation that a partner should be able to fill our love deficit. Help us stop thinking that there is something wrong with the partner because we are not getting the love we need.

Master Paul, love is an art,
it opens up the secret heart.
Master Paul, love's rushing flow,
my heart awash in sacred glow.

O Holy Spirit, flow through me,
I am the open door for thee.
O mighty rushing stream of Light,
transcendence is my sacred right.

4. Paul the Venetian, help us shift our attitude towards relationships so that we can focus on becoming aware of our own dysfunctional patterns and change them, instead of demanding that our partner should change.

Master Paul, accelerate,
upon pure love I meditate.
Master Paul, intentions pure,
my self-transcendence will ensure.

O Holy Spirit, flow through me,
I am the open door for thee.
O mighty rushing stream of Light,
transcendence is my sacred right.

5. Paul the Venetian, help us transcend the power game disguised as love where we are using the intellect to try to analyze a partner, and the purpose is to get the partner to change so that we do not have to change.

Master Paul, your love will heal,
my inner light you do reveal.
Master Paul, all life console,
with you I'm being truly whole.

O Holy Spirit, flow through me,
I am the open door for thee.
O mighty rushing stream of Light,
transcendence is my sacred right.

6. Paul the Venetian, help us see the futility of projecting that the problem is out there and that the solution must be that our partner changes. Help us overcome the illusion that we cannot change until the partner has changed.

Master Paul, you serve the All,
by helping us transcend the fall.
Master Paul, in peace we rise,
as ego meets its sure demise.

O Holy Spirit, flow through me,
I am the open door for thee.
O mighty rushing stream of Light,
transcendence is my sacred right.

7. Paul the Venetian, help us see that we will *not* save the relationship by focusing on the lacks of both of us. A successful relationship, where there is maximum creativity, can be based only on a focus on the whole.

Master Paul, love all life free,
your love is for eternity.
Master Paul, you are the One,
to help us make the journey fun.

O Holy Spirit, flow through me,
I am the open door for thee.
O mighty rushing stream of Light,
transcendence is my sacred right.

8. Paul the Venetian, help us see that a creative relationship can only happen when both partners are seeking to become open doors for their I AM Presences. We must overcome the patterns in our psychology so the Conscious You has no coloring from the outer self.

Master Paul, you balance all,
the seven rays upon my call.
Master Paul, you paint the sky,
with colors that delight the I.

O Holy Spirit, flow through me,
I am the open door for thee.
O mighty rushing stream of Light,
transcendence is my sacred right.

9. Paul the Venetian, help us connect to the Conscious You in ourselves and each other so we can allow the Conscious You the freedom to flow. Help us take the next step up and allow each other to be.

Master Paul, your Presence here,
filling up my inner sphere.
Life is now a sacred flow,
God Love I do on all bestow.

O Holy Spirit, flow through me,
I am the open door for thee.
O mighty rushing stream of Light,
transcendence is my sacred right.

4. We are in a creative relationship

1. Paul the Venetian, help us recognize that the purpose of a relationship is *not* to give both partners love. The purpose is to be creative and bring forth something that is more than each of us could bring forth alone.

Master Lanto, golden wise,
expose in me the ego's lies.
Master Lanto, will to be,
I will to win my mastery.

O Holy Spirit, flow through me,
I am the open door for thee.
O mighty rushing stream of Light,
transcendence is my sacred right.

2. Paul the Venetian, help us recognize that although we have a need for love, we will never receive enough love from our partner or any other human being. One cannot receive enough love from outside oneself but only from the I AM Presence.

Master Lanto, balance all,
for wisdom's balance I do call.
Master Lanto, help me see,
that balance is the Golden key.

O Holy Spirit, flow through me,
I am the open door for thee.
O mighty rushing stream of Light,
transcendence is my sacred right.

3. Paul the Venetian, help us accept that we each have a responsibility to establish a connection with our I AM Presence. This is not the responsibility of our partner or guru or an ascended master.

Master Lanto, from Above,
I call forth discerning love.
Master Lanto, love's not blind,
through love, God vision I will find.

O Holy Spirit, flow through me,
I am the open door for thee.
O mighty rushing stream of Light,
transcendence is my sacred right.

4. Paul the Venetian, help us grasp that we cannot receive the love we need from any external source but only from our I AM Presences.

Master Lanto, pure I am,
intentions pure as Christic lamb.
Master Lanto, I will transcend,
acceleration now my truest friend.

O Holy Spirit, flow through me,
I am the open door for thee.
O mighty rushing stream of Light,
transcendence is my sacred right.

5. Paul the Venetian, help us overcome the illusion that our ultimate fulfillment can come from establishing this otherworldly love relationship to the perfect partner here on earth.

Master Lanto, I am whole,
no more division in my soul.
Master Lanto, healing flame,
all balance in your sacred name.

O Holy Spirit, flow through me,
I am the open door for thee.
O mighty rushing stream of Light,
transcendence is my sacred right.

6. Paul the Venetian, help us grasp that our ultimate fulfillment can come only by establishing a relationship where the I AM Presence is the Alpha aspect of our beings and the Conscious You is the Omega aspect of our beings.

Master Lanto, serve all life,
as I transcend all inner strife.
Master Lanto, peace you give,
to all who want to truly live.

O Holy Spirit, flow through me,
I am the open door for thee.
O mighty rushing stream of Light,
transcendence is my sacred right.

7. Paul the Venetian, help us establish the correct figure-eight flow in our beings, the vertical figure-eight flow, and then establish a creative figure-eight flow with each other here on earth.

Master Lanto, free to be,
in balanced creativity.
Master Lanto, we employ,
your balance as the key to joy.

O Holy Spirit, flow through me,
I am the open door for thee.
O mighty rushing stream of Light,
transcendence is my sacred right.

8. Paul the Venetian, help us grasp that a man and a woman can be complete equals only when both recognize their relationship with the I AM Presence. Help us overcome all value judgments or comparisons so we can accept and nourish each others completeness.

Master Lanto, balance all,
the seven rays upon my call.
Master Lanto, I take flight,
my threefold flame a blazing light.

O Holy Spirit, flow through me,
I am the open door for thee.
O mighty rushing stream of Light,
transcendence is my sacred right.

9. Paul the Venetian, help us grasp that the relationship will find its most successful expression only if we allow both of us to fulfill our Divine plans. Help us see that a successful relationship is one where the two partners help each other go as far as possible on their individual journeys.

Lanto dear, your Presence here,
filling up my inner sphere.
Life is now a sacred flow,
God Wisdom I on all bestow.

**O Holy Spirit, flow through me,
I am the open door for thee.
O mighty rushing stream of Light,
transcendence is my sacred right.**

Sealing:

In the name of the Divine Mother, I fully accept that the power of these calls is used to set free the Ma-ter light, so it can outpicture the perfect vision of Christ for my own life, for all people and for the planet. In the name I AM THAT I AM, it is done! Amen.

8 | LOVE AND LOVE

Paul the Venetian I AM. We have now reached the third level of initiation at my retreat, that of love and love. When you get a double dose of love, what are you facing? First of all, you are facing the initiation of overcoming the subtle power game that is embedded in all forms of competition. What does competition have to do with love, you might say? It is a perversion of love. What is the core of love? It is the desire to be more, but the question is: "More than what?"

The essence of becoming more

We have for years given teachings on the concept of becoming more, of being more. We know well that when your outer analytical mind hears this, it can react in only one way. More means more than something. How do you know you have become more unless you can compare it to a previous state where you were less?

How do you measure more? Do you think Master MORE can be measured by any standard on earth? Many of you do because you have not yet tuned in to his Presence that is beyond compare, as is mine, as is your own I AM Presence.

There is a difference, a subtle but fundamental difference, between becoming more by flowing with the River of Life and becoming more according to some comparison in the material universe that is yet an unascended sphere. When you are becoming more by flowing with the River of Life, you are transcending your sense of self. What is the standard that you compare to? It is what you were before, what you were yesterday, a minute ago or a lifetime ago. You look back and you see: "I am now more than I was before." This is not competition. This is doing what comes naturally in the world of form: Measuring your progress, measuring the expansion of your sense of self. This is legitimate; it is necessary; it is constructive. The moment you begin comparing yourself, either to a standard defined on earth or to other people, then this is not constructive. It is a perversion of the drive to become more, which is the core of love.

How the fallen beings compete with God

Where does this perversion come from? It comes in its original form from the fallen beings who, when they decided that they knew better than God how the universe should function and how lifestreams should be saved, also decided (although without fully realizing this) that they were in a state of competition with God. Do you not see, with what we have told you about the fallen beings, that they are competing with God in the ultimate power game? [For more information, see *Cosmology of Evil.*]

Who has control of the universe? Who has ultimate power to say who is saved and who is not? Surely, the Creator has ultimate power. Those who are in oneness with the Creator and serve on the Karmic Board have power to say who is saved and who is not. The representatives of the Creator determine this only by looking at how you have transcended self. Have you transcended self to the point where you have transcended all selfishness and you are now working to raise the all? Then you are ready to ascend to the spiritual realm and become an ascended master. Until you have transcended that selfishness, you are not ready. This is not a punishment. It is not a judgment. It is as impossible for you to ascend as it is for a hot air balloon to rise into the air until it has enough upward momentum to overcome the downward pull of gravity on its mass.

The fallen beings have done something entirely different. They have created a standard that says: "You are not worthy to be saved unless you live up to this standard." They have created a false polarity where there is the standard as one extreme and then the opposite of the standard as the other extreme. It now becomes possible to compare people based on this standard and say: "Some people are right; some people are wrong. Some people are good; some people are evil. Some people are worthy of God's salvation. Some people are worthy to be condemned to hell for all eternity." This is what is behind competition on earth. There are many people on earth who are entirely caught up in this vain competition for some kind of glory on earth.

The will to improve yourself

There is a discernment to be made. It is entirely possible for all lifestreams on a given planet to go into a state of consciousness where they are not striving to improve themselves. You have been told that there are planets that have self-destructed because of war among the inhabitants of the planet. There are also planets that have self-destructed because the inhabitants of the planet entered such a homogeneous state of consciousness that none of them were trying to transcend their sense of self. They all validated each other in this state of complete mediocrity. The earth was, at some point in the past, in danger of entering such a spiral. That is why a diversity of lifestreams were allowed to embody here, including some fallen beings.

In order for you to rise from a lower state of consciousness to a higher state of consciousness, there must be a will, a will to do better than you have done before. While you are below the 48th level of consciousness, this will must have a motivation. What kind of motivation can you grasp when you are below the 48th level? You can grasp the desire for some kind of glory on earth, to be better than others, to win some kind of prize, to become famous, to become a hero, to be looked up to by others.

When you look at the world of sports, for example, I am not saying that all competition is completely wrong in an absolute sense. There are athletes who, through their competitiveness, have become so willing to transcend themselves that it has prepared them for discovering the spiritual path. This does not mean I am saying there is competition in heaven, or that competition is of God, or that we of the ascended masters condone or encourage competition. It means that on a planet with the state of consciousness of earth, it is a necessary device for helping people gain a motivation for improving themselves.

This can help people rise to the 48th level of consciousness where they discover something higher. I am not thereby saying that all athletes, or all who are engaging in some form of competition, are below the 48th level, but I *am* saying that the vast majority of them are below the 48th level. There are a few who have risen above it and who participate in the competition for other reasons, but the majority are certainly below and are motivated by competition as a comparative process. They are constantly comparing themselves to other people or to some standard, such as breaking the world record, winning the most tennis games, making the most money on your sport, or whatever you have that drives people.

Competition in personal relationships

The real problem with a competitive spirit is seen no more clearly than in your personal relationships. What is the highest outcome of any personal relationship, be it a love relationship or parents, siblings or children? What is the highest outcome of any human relationship? It is that both parties in the relationship come to the point where they are working to raise up each other, at the same time as they are walking the spiritual path of transcending themselves. This is the highest outcome. How will you ever rise to that level if you see yourself as being in competition with your brothers or sisters, even with your parents, with your spouse or with your co-workers or friends? If you are always trying to be better, to keep up with the Joneses, or even go beyond the Joneses, how will you get out of this competitive spirit and get into the Creative Spirit?

I have spoken about love relationships in my previous discourses, and let us look at them again. If you go back to the old role between men and women, there was not so much competition between the man and the wife. The woman had been brought up to accept her place and saw that there was no point in competing with the man.

This did lead to some relationships that were constructive. They were not constructive in the highest possible way, but they were still constructive in the sense that the woman had accepted that it was the husband who had a career or who had a job or position in society, and she was doing everything possible to help him fulfill that mission. At the same time, he was grateful for her support and was also doing everything possible to help her with her interests and her growth. There are quite a few relationships that were positive this way because there was no competition. Of course, this was, as I have already said, based on an unbalanced suppression of women that was not ultimately healthy or healthy in the long run. I am not condoning this. I am just giving it as an example of what can happen when there is no competition among the spouses.

What do you have in the modern age? You have had a process that has made some progress towards liberating women and giving them equality. We can discuss whether this process has given women full liberty and full equality, and I will be the first to say it has not, but that is not my issue here. My issue is that with the liberation of women, with women entering the workplace and getting careers, there has been an opening for competition among spouses, and it has ruined many love relationships.

You still have many cultures where the boys are brought up to be competitive in sports, in terms of making money and this and that. At the same time, the girls are also being brought up to pursue an education, a job, a career. The boy is not aware of what it means that he now marries a woman who is not like his mother who accepted her place. He expects that his wife is going to do everything that his mother did in the home while still working. This, of course, can only lead to conflict.

At the same time, many women feel that they have a double pressure. They are supposed to go out and get a career and do whatever it takes to be successful in the workplace, but they are also supposed to be the perfect wife, mother and housekeeper at home. How can anyone do this? It is impossible; the men certainly could not do that.

Many women have tried, tried hard, and have found that they could not. Many have lost their confidence. Many have become frustrated, traumatized by this process. Many marriages have broken up because of this frustration from both sides. What you have seen over the last several decades in the modern, industrialized world is that, as the old roles of the two sexes have been broken up, people have struggled mightily to find a new way to relate to each other in a relationship.

Overcoming competition

When you come to the third level at my retreat, I and my assistants will help you take a look at yourself and see whether you are still affected by competitiveness. We will especially help you see whether you have a competition with your spouse or just a tendency for this even if you do not have a spouse. It is essential that you overcome this competition, not only for your own growth, but also for your potential to have a constructive love relationship.

What is the key to beginning to overcome this competitiveness? It is to contemplate that the only real "competition" is in terms of transcending your sense of self. You can compare with how you were in the past and see that you have made progress, but what is progress? It is not in some kind of skill, ability or position on earth. It is certainly not in the numbers on your bank account. It is a matter of how much you are the open door for your I AM Presence.

When you begin to realize this, you can see that it gives no meaning to compare yourself to others, especially not to your spouse. Does it really matter who makes the most money? Does it matter who has the highest position or the most recognition? It will not matter when you realize a very profound truth.

A dangerous perversion of love

The fallen beings have attempted to pervert love in many ways, but there is probably not a more dangerous perversion than the idea that in order to deserve God's love, you need to live up to a standard defined on earth. They want you to believe that there is a God in heaven and he is a loving God. God loves you, but in order to receive God's love, you have to deserve it. In order to deserve it, you have to live up to a standard defined by the fallen beings.

Is this logical, my beloved? The fallen beings have no love. They cannot produce love. You cannot produce love; you can receive it from above. You may use this as a mantra:

> I cannot produce love;
> I can only receive it from above.

What sense does it make that those who have no love, and who have turned their backs on God's love, can define a standard that, in a mechanical way, means that God will automatically give you love if you live up to this standard? It makes no sense whatsoever.

I can argue all day and all night and give you reasons in order to try to make your analytical mind fathom God's love, but what did I say in my last discourse about the analytical mind? It cannot deal with infinity because it is a comparative mind. It compares everything to what it already knows or to some standard, and then it analyzes by breaking things down into components. On earth, you can take a certain form and break it down into components, and you can get down to what seems to be the ultimate component, at least in the material frequency spectrum.

Love is not physical! It is not a thing; it cannot be broken into components. It has no components. You may say: "But does not love have certain expressions? Is not love such and such or so and so?" I would say: "Love has no components. Love has no expression."

It is when love is distorted by the outer mind that it takes on certain characteristics. What most people call love is not love at all, and it is because they have colored love. What people are expressing is often far better than when they are expressing pure evil or completely fear-based feelings. There are certain human feelings that are clearly of a higher vibration than certain other human feelings. Some of what human beings call love has a higher vibration than human anger or hatred. Nevertheless, it is a human, comparable, relative feeling, and *that* is not pure love—it is not *Divine* love.

Your analytical, outer mind will never be able to fathom love, the true nature of Divine love. Your outer mind will want love to be something that it can deal with by describing its characteristics, analyzing its components and comparing it to its standard for truth. I could attempt to come up with arguments for why love, Divine love, really is the way it is, but your outer mind could come up with counter arguments for why love cannot be the way it is.

How *is* Divine love? The truth that the outer mind will never be able to fathom, and that the ego will never be able to accept, is that Divine love is completely and utterly beyond conditions. We may call it unconditional love because it is the shortest expression that somewhat describes Divine love. It is beyond any condition that could be defined by the consciousness of relativity and separation. That is why it cannot be compared to any thing on earth. It cannot be fit into any standard. It cannot be fit into a definition.

Experiencing the unconditionality of Divine love

I could give you arguments for this, but I do not intend to because when you are participating in this course, you are going to my retreat at night. At my retreat I have several methods for helping you experience unconditional love, and when you have this experience it is not a matter of arguing for or against it. The question is: "Can you translate the experience of unconditional love that you have at my retreat, in that greater purity of the etheric octave, through your conscious mind?" Your conscious mind is often focused in the material world, which is a lower vibration than the etheric octave. It is far more difficult to experience unconditional love with the conscious mind.

Many of you have experienced, at least in glimpses, unconditional love or some state of unconditional or pure consciousness. Many of you have had mystical experiences, and then it is just a matter of realizing that this shows you something about love. It is a matter of opening up your mind and your heart, setting aside your mental images of what love is until you can have that conscious experience.

I know well that there are people who will argue against the idea that Divine love is unconditional. There are even ascended master students, or at least *former* ascended master students, who will argue against this. By arguing against it, you are closing your outer mind to the conscious experience of it. If you choose that you do not want to experience Divine love, I respect your choice, but then I must question why you set yourself up as an expert on love? How can you be an expert on love if you will not experience love in its highest facet? Can this really make sense to anyone, my beloved?

Divine love is not conditional or controllable

Those who are the most eager to set themselves up as experts or authority figures on earth are those who are most trapped in the fallen consciousness. They want to control everything, and the fallen beings most certainly want to control love. They want to shut out Divine love. They want to prevent all spiritual people from acknowledging, accepting, and experiencing unconditional love. They desperately want to keep you believing that love is conditional and can be defined by their standard.

Love, my beloved, is beyond words, beyond forms and beyond images. It cannot be defined. It cannot be owned. It cannot be controlled. You can either be an open door for love to stream through you, or you will cut yourself off from it. What have I said about ownership? You want to stop the clock. You want everything to stand still so you can own that which you think you need to own. What is Divine love? Why is it unconditional? What does it mean that something is unconditional? It means it never stands still. It is always flowing on and transcending itself. That is why it cannot be captured in any form.

Love is that which always pulls you to become more, to transcend yourself, so that you come closer and closer to oneness with your I AM Presence and to your ascension. If you think that you can stop the flow of love and create a mental image and project it upon love and say: "This is what love is," then you have absolutely no idea what love is.

Love cannot be captured. It cannot be owned. The ego will never accept this. The fallen beings will never accept this, unless they are awakened somehow, which the fallen beings *can* be, but the ego *cannot*.

This should not trouble you when you are engaging in the path to self-mastery. Your concern should be to look honestly at your outer mind, at your upbringing, at how you have been conditioned to have a certain mental image of what love is and is not. You need to question those standards so that you free your mind from this attachment to a certain image of love. That way, you open up your conscious mind to experience what your etheric mind has already experienced.

Making the experience of unconditional love conscious

In both cases, it is the Conscious You that experiences. For you, the Conscious You, to experience unconditional love at the conscious level, and to retain conscious awareness of this experience, you need to have a certain separation from the separate mind. You need to distance yourself from these false images, these fallen images, of love. It is not my intent here to give you arguments that convince your outer mind that love really is unconditional. It is my intent to help you have, with the conscious mind, a conscious recognition and awareness of what you have experienced at my retreat in the etheric realm.

What can we do in my retreat to help you have this experience of unconditional love? We use the device I talked about earlier where we can make visible on a screen what happens in your energy field at subconscious levels. We can show you how you have perverted love and used it to build prison walls around your conscious mind. We can show you how this ties you to the fallen beings, to the collective consciousness, to the astral plane.

When you see this, you will often be shocked at first. You will be shocked at seeing how much of the energy that comes from your I AM Presence is directed into a perversion of love. You will be shocked at seeing how much of that energy is then sucked in by demons and entities in the astral plane. You will be shocked at seeing these reservoirs of perverted energy. You will be shocked at seeing the incredibly inharmonious and ugly beings who reside in those reservoirs and who have their claws and their hooks into your energy field through these perversions of love. [For more information about this, see *Cosmology of Evil*.]

When you see this visually at the etheric level, then you are motivated to look at your own subconscious mind and discover the beliefs that cause you to pervert love. You are willing to look at these mental images of love that come from the fallen mind and that you have accepted. There is no blame for you accepting this. How is it possible to grow up on a planet like earth, or to live here for lifetimes, without accepting these perversions of love that are so pervasive on this planet?

I have no desire to put you down, and you know this at the etheric level because you experience it directly. When you read this at the conscious level, your outer mind may still not experience my Presence and vibration the same way you would if I stood next to you physically. When you are at my retreat in the etheric realm, you do experience my Being, my Presence. You know, you *experience,* that I have no blame. What you feel coming from me is precisely the unconditional love that only wants to raise you up.

When I show you how you are tied to these forces of anti-love, you are not feeling that I am criticizing or putting you down. You are only experiencing that I want you to be free, but also that you can be free only when you *see*. You must *see* how you are tied to the forces of anti-love. You must *see* why you are tied to them through your incorrect beliefs and mental images about love. It is when you make love conditional that you tie yourself to the conditional beings who long ago fell out of oneness with Spirit.

The ego will reject unconditional love

I have earlier spoken about a love relationship where you expect that your partner is going to give you the love you need. I have said that it is *your* responsibility to get that love from within yourself, from your I AM Presence. You will not be able to get that love, to *accept* that love, until you begin to contemplate and accept consciously that love is unconditional.

If you see God as conditional, you will reject unconditional love. You will not recognize it as love because it does not live up to your conditions, to your definition of love so you think it is something else. Perhaps, you even feel threatened by it. Certainly, your ego feels threatened by it. If you identify with this, you will reject love.

In the etheric realm, in my retreat, there are still students who come and when they experience my love, they reject it. They recoil in horror sometimes, but then I can also show them on the screen what effect this has, where it comes from and what the belief is. I can show them what happens in your energy field when a ray of unconditional love flows into it. I can show you how your ego recoils in absolute horror, in absolute hatred, against this love and does everything possible to reject it. It ties itself into a knot in order to get you to reject unconditional love. When you see it visually, most students will immediately snap out of it at the etheric level. What I aim to do with this book, that speaks to your conscious mind, is to facilitate the process whereby you can also accept this at the conscious level.

When you are in a love relationship, you are meant to get love from your spouse, but how will you get love from your spouse if you have so many conditions for how you define love? In my retreat I can show you how, in the vast majority of relationships on earth, one or both partners are rejecting the love coming from the other. Men are not from Mars and women are not from Venus, but because of the extremely unbalanced state between the sexes that has been so dominant on this earth for thousands of years, boys and girls are brought up with different views of love and feelings, how you express feelings and how you deal with feelings. In so many love relationships, the woman is more free to express love and can express it more unconditionally than the man, but in most cases the man cannot accept this love. He has been brought up with a different image of how love should be expressed, and he cannot handle that the wife expresses it more freely or expresses a higher form of love.

On the other hand, most women have a severe problem when they are expressing their love and when they feel it is not received. They feel rejected, they feel worthless, they feel ignored. After feeling rejected by the husband, the woman starts feeling that the husband is not expressing enough love towards her. Of course, the woman has been brought up to think that the husband should express love the same way she does, but how can he when he was brought up with an entirely different view of love? It is almost unavoidable that both are disappointed. You often see the pattern where the woman starts feeling that she is not loved enough, and she starts accusing her husband: "You don't love me anymore. You don't love me enough. You never express love. You never say it."

When that happens, the man can in most cases only react by feeling inadequate. Perhaps, he even has some awareness that he is not able to express love freely. He senses that his wife is missing something that he cannot give. Because he doesn't know how to give it, he feels inadequate and he wants his wife to stop accusing him. He goes into a pattern of either frantically trying to show his love as best he can, hoping it will be enough, or he just denies the whole thing and starts withdrawing more and more from the wife, trying to stop her from being so emotional.

There is only one solution to this, and it is that both husband and wife must go through the individual process of overcoming the perversions of love that they have been brought up to accept. They must begin to accept unconditional love from their I AM Presences. As you open yourself up to feeling the love from your I AM Presence, you will also begin to be able to express it, if you are willing to try and to continue to try.

Unconditional love does not stand still

I have said that love will not stand still so how can you experience love when you are in embodiment on earth? Some of you will have experienced that you can go into deep meditation or an inner sense of oneness, and you can experience unconditional love coming from your I AM Presence, an ascended master or God. You have also experienced that, in most cases, you cannot carry this love with you in your normal, daily, waking consciousness and activities.

Why is this? It is because, when you have the experience of love, this is meant as a gift for you to open yourself up to letting love flow through you. You can have a genuine, mystical experience of unconditional love, but it is only meant to give you a sense of co-measurement of what love is. Then you need to take the next step, just as Jesus explained in his parable about the servants who were given talents. The two servants multiplied the talents, and the third one buried them in the ground. Do not bury your love in the ground but dare to express it.

You cannot on a continual basis experience love unless you express it, unless you let if flow through you. The only way to experience love continually is to let it flow through your chakras, your mind, your being, your words and your actions. Love wants to be expressed. It wants to flow. You cannot experience unconditional love as a static state. You can experience this in a glimpse, but you cannot experience it on a continual basis. On a continual basis, you can experience love only as a stream, as a flow. How can there be flow unless there is an opening that it can flow through, unless there is a place it can flow into?

A dysfunctional pattern in relationships

The purpose of you expressing love towards your spouse is not to get a certain reaction from your spouse. This is one of the most dysfunctional patterns in relationships. One spouse has some awareness of unconditional love and begins to express that love towards the other spouse, but then it is not received as expected, maybe because the other spouse is not yet ready to accept unconditional love. The first spouse feels that the love is rejected. Maybe you feel that *you* have been rejected, and then you start stopping the flow of love. You cut off the flow. You are tying the expression of your love to how your partner receives it.

My beloved, here is where you need to recognize that sometimes egoism is not as bad as it is made out to be. There is a point on the spiritual path where you need to have a higher form of egoism and say: "What is best for me? What is best for my spiritual growth here? Is it best for me that I make this effort, that I have this grace of having an experience of unconditional love, and then I express it towards my spouse? When my spouse cannot receive it as I think it should be received, then I react by shutting off the flow. Is this really best for me, for my growth?"

Well, of course, it isn't, my beloved! Surely, you can see this! What *is* best for you? It is that you disconnect the expression of your love from how it is received or not received by your partner. You are not letting your expression of love be dependent on the state of mind and the choices of any other human being. You continue to express love, and you continue to expand your ability to express love.

One of two things will happen if you do this. Either your spouse will gradually be transformed so that he or she will be able to accept love, or you will continue to raise your consciousness until you can no longer stay in that relationship. You will be taken by the flow of love to another relationship where you can more freely express your love and where it can possibly be received more freely.

Be free in expressing your love

Another dysfunctional pattern is that you start expressing love and you expect that your spouse should reciprocate by also expressing love to you. Again, your spouse may not be ready for this, or in some cases may not be willing. You may attempt to talk to your spouse about both receiving and expressing love, but if that does not produce any results, focus on expanding the flow of love through yourself, expanding your ability to be an open door for love. Expand your willingness to express it in ever more refined, ever more free, ways. The more free you can be in expressing love, the more you will free yourself from any ties to a person or situation where love cannot be freely expressed. The more you express love, the more you build the momentum that will eventually gain critical mass until it carries you out of that situation and into a situation where love can more freely be expressed.

Am I hereby saying that you should consciously, with your outer mind, decide to leave your spouse if your spouse cannot receive or express love. Nay, that is not what I am saying. I am saying to open yourself up to the flow of unconditional love. If you have conditions and apply them to how your spouse should receive or express love, then you are not opening yourself up to the flow of unconditional love.

Do not think that you can get away with using my teaching as a convenient excuse for leaving a spouse. At least, do not think you can fool *me* by doing this. Focus on opening yourself to the flow of unconditional love. Stay in the relationship until you get some undeniable demonstration from above that it is time to flow on. Do not decide with the outer mind.

In fact, resist the outer mind's attempts at getting you to make such a decision. Learn to recognize when you feel a decision is being forced by the ego. Then resist this; refuse to make that decision. Learn to recognize that sometimes there is a subtle shift in awareness where you feel that some tie, some rope that ties you to the shore just lets go. You feel you are free to flow with the stream of life.

Love relationships are a great challenge

My beloved, you may be beginning to realize that, when you come to my retreat of the Third Ray of Love, one of the primary things you will be working on is your love relationships. One of the greatest challenges that you face on the spiritual path is your love relationships. I have already given you hints at the very fact that planet earth is a planet where the relationship between man and woman has been so perverted, has become so unbalanced, that it is extremely difficult to have a high relationship, a creative relationship.

There are so many forces that seek to destroy relationships because there is hardly a more efficient way to delay people's spiritual progress. Well, there *are* more efficient ways, such as getting people to go to war where they are killed or wounded either physically or psychologically. In what you call "normal life situations," love relationships have caused many people to delay their spiritual progress, or even to abort it completely, by going into some destructive pattern of fighting with their spouse, or seeking to destroy the spouse that cannot be controlled.

I am not, in any way, wishing you to start blaming yourself if you have not been successful in relationships. On the contrary, I am seeking to give you a sense of co-measurement that having a love relationship on planet earth is a very big challenge. There are other planets where it is so much easier that you would scarcely believe it. Have some forgiveness of yourself if you have had issues or problems in relationships. Make an effort to have forgiveness and patience with your spouse.

Forgiving your partner and moving on

If you have experienced relationships that ended, then realize one thing: The only thing you can do is to *move on*. In order to move on, you have to be willing to learn the lessons you need to learn from that relationship. You also need to forgive, to set your spouse free from all guilt or blame.

I know well that your ego will react to this and say: "But my spouse did this, that or the next thing. How can I forgive him or her?" You are not forgiving in order to let the *other* person off the hook. You are forgiving in order to let *yourself* off the hook, the hook that the fallen beings have in your consciousness through your non-forgiveness.

You need to have the conscious awareness that what is best for your growth is that you move on from any relationship that has ended. In order to move on, you need to forgive. You need to forgive your spouse, but you also need to forgive yourself. You need to just *let go*.

There is a rope that ties you to the past, that keeps your boat in a turbulent place in the River of Life. Reach down deep into your emotional body and feel how the rope is tied in a knot. Loosen the knot so that you are holding the rope in your hand and just open your hand and let go. Feel how the boat of your outer vehicle, your soul vehicle, now is free to flow down the stream where you quickly flow out of the turbulence and into a calmer stretch of the river.

I AM Paul the Venetian and love is my greatest love. My next-greatest love is *you*.

9 | I INVOKE FREE-FLOWING LOVE

In the name I AM THAT I AM, Jesus Christ, I call to my I AM Presence to flow through the I Will Be Presence that I AM and give this invocation with full power. I call to beloved Elohim Heros and Amora, Archangel Chamuel and Charity and Paul the Venetian to help us accept that Divine love is beyond conditions so we can both express and receive love on earth. Help us see and surrender all patterns that block our oneness with Paul the Venetian and with our I AM Presences, including …

[Make personal calls]

1. We overcome all competition

1. Paul the Venetian, help us overcome the subtle power game of competition. Help us see how the ego takes love and the drive to be more and perverts it into wanting to be more than other people.

O Heros-Amora, in your love so pink,
I care not what others about me may think,
in oneness with you, I claim a new day,
an innocent child, I frolic and play.

O Heros-Amora, a new life begun,
I laugh at the devil, the serious one,
I bathe in your glorious Ruby-Pink Sun,
knowing my God allows life to be fun.

2. Paul the Venetian, help us grasp the subtle but fundamental difference between becoming more by flowing with the River of Life and becoming more according to some comparison in this world.

O Heros-Amora, life is such a joy,
I see that the world is like a great toy,
whatever my mind into it projects,
the mirror of life exactly reflects.

O Heros-Amora, I reap what I sow,
yet this is Plan B for helping me grow,
for truly, Plan A is that I join the flow,
immersed in the Infinite Love you bestow.

3. Paul the Venetian, help us grasp that when one is flowing with the River of Life, one is transcending the sense of self and cannot compare oneself to other people.

O Heros-Amora, conditions you burn,
I know I AM free to take a new turn,
Immersed in the stream of infinite Love,
I know that my Spirit came from Above.

O Heros-Amora, awakened I see,
in true love is no conditionality,
the devil is stuck in his duality,
but I AM set free by Love's reality.

4. Paul the Venetian, help us overcome the vain competition for some glory on earth. Help us especially overcome all tendency to compete with the people closest to us.

O Heros-Amora, I feel that at last,
I've risen above the trap of my past,
in true love I claim my freedom to grow,
forever I'm one with Love's Infinite Flow.

O Heros-Amora, conditions are ties,
forming a net of serpentine lies,
your love has no bounds, forever it flies,
raising all life into Ruby-Pink skies.

5. Paul the Venetian, help us grasp that the highest outcome of any personal relationship is that both parties are working to raise up each other while walking the spiritual path.

O Heros-Amora, in your love so pink,
I care not what others about me may think,
in oneness with you, I claim a new day,
an innocent child, I frolic and play.

O Heros-Amora, a new life begun,
I laugh at the devil, the serious one,
I bathe in your glorious Ruby-Pink Sun,
knowing my God allows life to be fun.

6. Paul the Venetian, help us get out of the competitive spirit and get into the Creative Spirit. Help us overcome all competition between us.

> O Heros-Amora, life is such a joy,
> I see that the world is like a great toy,
> whatever my mind into it projects,
> the mirror of life exactly reflects.
>
> **O Heros-Amora, I reap what I sow,**
> **yet this is Plan B for helping me grow,**
> **for truly, Plan A is that I join the flow,**
> **immersed in the Infinite Love you bestow.**

7. Paul the Venetian, help us overcome the old roles for men and women and accept that we both have Divine plans and active lives. Help us support instead of competing with each other.

> O Heros-Amora, conditions you burn,
> I know I AM free to take a new turn,
> Immersed in the stream of infinite Love,
> I know that my Spirit came from Above.
>
> **O Heros-Amora, awakened I see,**
> **in true love is no conditionality,**
> **the devil is stuck in his duality,**
> **but I AM set free by Love's reality.**

8. Paul the Venetian, help us overcome the piscean roles and find the aquarian way to relate to each other.

O Heros-Amora, I feel that at last,
I've risen above the trap of my past,
in true love I claim my freedom to grow,
forever I'm one with Love's Infinite Flow.

O Heros-Amora, conditions are ties,
forming a net of serpentine lies,
your love has no bounds, forever it flies,
raising all life into Ruby-Pink skies.

9. Paul the Venetian, help us overcome all competition about who makes the most money, who has the highest position or the most recognition.

Accelerate into Oneness, I AM real,
Accelerate into Oneness, all life heal,
Accelerate into Oneness, I AM MORE,
Accelerate into Oneness, all will soar.

Accelerate into Oneness! (3X)
Beloved Heros and Amora.
Accelerate into Oneness! (3X)
Beloved Chamuel and Charity.
Accelerate into Oneness! (3X)
Beloved Paul the Venetian.
Accelerate into Oneness! (3X)
Beloved I AM.

2. We experience unconditional love

1. Paul the Venetian, help us overcome the illusion that in order to deserve God's love we need to live up to a standard defined on earth.

Chamuel Archangel, in ruby ray power,
I know I am taking a life-giving shower.
Love burning away all perversions of will,
I suddenly feel my desires falling still.

Chamuel Archangel, descend from Above,
Chamuel Archangel, with ruby-pink love,
Chamuel Archangel, so often thought-of,
Chamuel Archangel, o come Holy Dove.

2. Paul the Venetian, help us see that we cannot produce love, we can only receive it from above.

Chamuel Archangel, a spiral of light,
as ruby ray fire now pierces the night.
All forces of darkness consumed by your fire,
consuming all those who will not rise higher.

Chamuel Archangel, descend from Above,
Chamuel Archangel, with ruby-pink love,
Chamuel Archangel, so often thought-of,
Chamuel Archangel, o come Holy Dove.

3. Paul the Venetian, help us see that what most people call love is not love at all because they have colored love.

Chamuel Archangel, your love so immense,
with clarified vision, my life now makes sense.
The purpose of life you so clearly reveal,
immersed in your love, God's oneness I feel.

Chamuel Archangel, descend from Above,
Chamuel Archangel, with ruby-pink love,
Chamuel Archangel, so often thought-of,
Chamuel Archangel, o come Holy Dove.

4. Paul the Venetian, help us see that the analytical mind and the ego will never be able to fathom that Divine love is beyond any condition defined by the consciousness of relativity and separation.

Chamuel Archangel, what calmness you bring,
I see now that even death has no sting.
For truly, in love there can be no decay,
as love is transcendence into a new day.

Chamuel Archangel, descend from Above,
Chamuel Archangel, with ruby-pink love,
Chamuel Archangel, so often thought-of,
Chamuel Archangel, o come Holy Dove.

5. Paul the Venetian, help us experience unconditional love with our conscious minds. Help us set aside our mental images of love and open our minds and hearts to the conscious experience.

Chamuel Archangel, in ruby ray power,
I know I am taking a life-giving shower.
Love burning away all perversions of will,
I suddenly feel my desires falling still.

Chamuel Archangel, descend from Above,
Chamuel Archangel, with ruby-pink love,
Chamuel Archangel, so often thought-of,
Chamuel Archangel, o come Holy Dove.

6. Paul the Venetian, help us experience and accept that love cannot be defined, it cannot be owned it cannot be controlled. You can either be an open door for love to stream through you, or you will cut yourself off from it.

Chamuel Archangel, a spiral of light,
as ruby ray fire now pierces the night.
All forces of darkness consumed by your fire,
consuming all those who will not rise higher.

Chamuel Archangel, descend from Above,
Chamuel Archangel, with ruby-pink love,
Chamuel Archangel, so often thought-of,
Chamuel Archangel, o come Holy Dove.

7. Paul the Venetian, help us grasp that love is unconditional because it never stands still, it is always flowing and transcending itself. Love pulls us to transcend ourselves so that we come closer to oneness with our I AM Presences.

Chamuel Archangel, your love so immense,
with clarified vision, my life now makes sense.
The purpose of life you so clearly reveal,
immersed in your love, God's oneness I feel.

Chamuel Archangel, descend from Above,
Chamuel Archangel, with ruby-pink love,
Chamuel Archangel, so often thought-of,
Chamuel Archangel, o come Holy Dove.

8. Paul the Venetian, help us overcome all false images of love. Show us how we have perverted love and used it to build prison walls around our conscious minds.

Chamuel Archangel, what calmness you bring,
I see now that even death has no sting.
For truly, in love there can be no decay,
as love is transcendence into a new day.

Chamuel Archangel, descend from Above,
Chamuel Archangel, with ruby-pink love,
Chamuel Archangel, so often thought-of,
Chamuel Archangel, o come Holy Dove.

9. Paul the Venetian, help us discover the beliefs that cause us to pervert love. Help us see the mental images of love that come from the fallen mind and that we have accepted.

With angels I soar,
as I reach for MORE.
The angels so real,
their love all will heal.
The angels bring peace,
all conflicts will cease.
With angels of light,
we soar to new height.

The rustling sound of angel wings,
what joy as even matter sings,
what joy as every atom rings,
in harmony with angel wings.

3. We express love unconditionally

1. Paul the Venetian, help us experience your Presence and know that you have no blame. Help us see how we are tied to the forces of anti-love by the illusions that make love conditional.

Master Paul, venetian dream,
your love for beauty's flowing stream.
Master Paul, in love's own womb,
your power shatters ego's tomb.

O Holy Spirit, flow through me,
I am the open door for thee.
O mighty rushing stream of Light,
transcendence is my sacred right.

2. Paul the Venetian, help us stop rejecting unconditional love by demanding that it should live up to our images of conditional love. Help us allow unconditional love to flow through us.

Master Paul, your counsel wise,
my mind is raised to lofty skies.
Master Paul, in wisdom's love,
such beauty flowing from Above.

O Holy Spirit, flow through me,
I am the open door for thee.
O mighty rushing stream of Light,
transcendence is my sacred right.

3. Paul the Venetian, help us see how our egos recoil in horror when they experience unconditional love. Help us see how the ego ties itself into a knot to get us to reject unconditional love. Help us snap out of this rejection at the conscious level.

Master Paul, love is an art,
it opens up the secret heart.
Master Paul, love's rushing flow,
my heart awash in sacred glow.

O Holy Spirit, flow through me,
I am the open door for thee.
O mighty rushing stream of Light,
transcendence is my sacred right.

4. Paul the Venetian, help us overcome the tendency to reject the love coming from each other. Help us see that we have different ways of expressing love so we can stop rejecting each other.

Master Paul, accelerate,
upon pure love I meditate.
Master Paul, intentions pure,
my self-transcendence will ensure.

O Holy Spirit, flow through me,
I am the open door for thee.
O mighty rushing stream of Light,
transcendence is my sacred right.

5. Paul the Venetian, help us overcome the tendency of one feeling the other does not express enough love whereby both of us go into a state of tension or blame that shuts down the flow between us.

Master Paul, your love will heal,
my inner light you do reveal.
Master Paul, all life console,
with you I'm being truly whole.

O Holy Spirit, flow through me,
I am the open door for thee.
O mighty rushing stream of Light,
transcendence is my sacred right.

6. Paul the Venetian, help us come to the point where we do not bury our love in the ground but dare to express it and let it flow through us.

Master Paul, you serve the All,
by helping us transcend the fall.
Master Paul, in peace we rise,
as ego meets its sure demise.

O Holy Spirit, flow through me,
I am the open door for thee.
O mighty rushing stream of Light,
transcendence is my sacred right.

7. Paul the Venetian, help us see that the purpose of expressing love towards a spouse is not to get a certain reaction from the spouse. Help us disconnect the expression of love from how it is received or not received by the partner.

Master Paul, love all life free,
your love is for eternity.
Master Paul, you are the One,
to help us make the journey fun.

O Holy Spirit, flow through me,
I am the open door for thee.
O mighty rushing stream of Light,
transcendence is my sacred right.

8. Paul the Venetian, help us focus on expanding the flow of love through ourselves. Help us expand our ability to be an open door for love and express it in ever-more refined and free ways.

Master Paul, you balance all,
the seven rays upon my call.
Master Paul, you paint the sky,
with colors that delight the I.

O Holy Spirit, flow through me,
I am the open door for thee.
O mighty rushing stream of Light,
transcendence is my sacred right.

9. Paul the Venetian, help us open ourselves to the flow of unconditional love by overcoming our conditions for how our spouse should receive or express love.

Master Paul, your Presence here,
filling up my inner sphere.
Life is now a sacred flow,
God Love I do on all bestow.

O Holy Spirit, flow through me,
I am the open door for thee.
O mighty rushing stream of Light,
transcendence is my sacred right.

4. We are moving on

1. Paul the Venetian, help us overcome the tendency to make decisions with the outer mind. Help us learn to recognize when a decision is forced by the ego. Help us make the subtle shift in awareness where we let go and are free to flow with the stream of life.

Master Paul, venetian dream,
your love for beauty's flowing stream.
Master Paul, in love's own womb,
your power shatters ego's tomb.

O Holy Spirit, flow through me,
I am the open door for thee.
O mighty rushing stream of Light,
transcendence is my sacred right.

2. Paul the Venetian, help us accept that one of the greatest challenges we face on the spiritual path is our love relationships.

Master Paul, your counsel wise,
my mind is raised to lofty skies.
Master Paul, in wisdom's love,
such beauty flowing from Above.

O Holy Spirit, flow through me,
I am the open door for thee.
O mighty rushing stream of Light,
transcendence is my sacred right.

3. Paul the Venetian, help us see that on planet earth the relationship between man and woman has become so unbalanced that it is difficult to have a creative relationship.

Master Paul, love is an art,
it opens up the secret heart.
Master Paul, love's rushing flow,
my heart awash in sacred glow.

O Holy Spirit, flow through me,
I am the open door for thee.
O mighty rushing stream of Light,
transcendence is my sacred right.

4. Paul the Venetian, help us see that there are many forces that seek to destroy relationships because there is hardly a more efficient way to delay our spiritual progress.

Master Paul, accelerate,
upon pure love I meditate.
Master Paul, intentions pure,
my self-transcendence will ensure.

O Holy Spirit, flow through me,
I am the open door for thee.
O mighty rushing stream of Light,
transcendence is my sacred right.

5. Paul the Venetian, help us see how love relationships have caused many people to stop their growth by going into a destructive pattern of fighting with a spouse or seeking to destroy a spouse that cannot be controlled.

Master Paul, your love will heal,
my inner light you do reveal.
Master Paul, all life console,
with you I'm being truly whole.

O Holy Spirit, flow through me,
I am the open door for thee.
O mighty rushing stream of Light,
transcendence is my sacred right.

6. Paul the Venetian, help us have forgiveness and patience with ourselves and each other concerning both our present and former love relationships.

Master Paul, you serve the All,
by helping us transcend the fall.
Master Paul, in peace we rise,
as ego meets its sure demise.

O Holy Spirit, flow through me,
I am the open door for thee.
O mighty rushing stream of Light,
transcendence is my sacred right.

7. Paul the Venetian, help us accept that when a relationship ends, the only thing we can do is to move on. Help us learn the lessons we need to learn from all of our relationships.

Master Paul, love all life free,
your love is for eternity.
Master Paul, you are the One,
to help us make the journey fun.

O Holy Spirit, flow through me,
I am the open door for thee.
O mighty rushing stream of Light,
transcendence is my sacred right.

8. Paul the Venetian, help us grasp the importance of forgiving our present and former spouses and set them free from all guilt or blame. Help us grasp that we are forgiving in order to set ourselves free from the hooks that the fallen beings have in our minds through our non-forgiveness.

Master Paul, you balance all,
the seven rays upon my call.
Master Paul, you paint the sky,
with colors that delight the I.

O Holy Spirit, flow through me,
I am the open door for thee.
O mighty rushing stream of Light,
transcendence is my sacred right.

9. Paul the Venetian, help us forgive ourselves. Help us reach into the emotional body, feel how the rope is tied in a knot, loosen the knot and let go and feel how we are free to flow with the River of Life.

Master Paul, your Presence here,
filling up my inner sphere.
Life is now a sacred flow,
God Love I do on all bestow.

O Holy Spirit, flow through me,
I am the open door for thee.
O mighty rushing stream of Light,
transcendence is my sacred right.

Sealing:

In the name of the Divine Mother, I fully accept that the power of these calls is used to set free the Ma-ter light, so it can outpicture the perfect vision of Christ for my own life, for all people and for the planet. In the name I AM THAT I AM, it is done! Amen.

10 | LOVE AND PURITY

I AM Paul the Venetian, Chohan of the Third Ray. Why is it so important that, at the third level of initiation at my retreat, you experience unconditional love? Why is it so important that you start having some conscious awareness of unconditional love and that you are loved unconditionally? It is important because it prepares you to handle the initiations at the fourth level where you encounter the energies of love combined with the Fourth Ray of Purity. Purity is always a special challenge for students on the spiritual path.

The initiations of the Fourth Ray

The first three rays are very much a preparation that is meant to take you to the point where you can handle the initiations of purity. The central challenge with purity is that when you encounter the Fourth Ray, its piercing, white light exposes with great clarity the impurities in your being. It is very possible that, upon seeing the impurities that you have not been able and willing to see before, you become greatly disturbed. You might begin to feel that because you have such impurities, how could you ever be redeemed? When you have experienced that God's love is unconditional, you will know that whatever impurities you discover in your being, you could never lose God's unconditional love.

The impurities that you discover can only be conditions in the material world. How can any conditions in the material world make you unworthy of receiving the love that is beyond all conditions and comes from a higher world? I know you can understand this intellectually, but until you experience that love is unconditional, you will not be ready for the initiations at the fourth level. Of course, I will not allow you to have those initiations until I know you are ready to handle them without going into a spiral of self-condemnation.

The inevitable pain of seeing an impurity

As much as I would like to make the path easier for you, I must also say that at the fourth level there is a certain inevitability that comes into play. One of the impurities that you have in your being is precisely the tendency to condemn yourself, to judge and put yourself down. You have this in your being if you have lived and grown up on planet earth. It cannot be any other way because this planet is so heavily infused with the judgmental consciousness of the fallen beings. You all have it when you come to my retreat. There is no way around this.

When you discover that you have the tendency to judge, it is almost inevitable that you will judge yourself for having this impurity of judging. You are not entirely free of the consciousness. Do you see this, my beloved? Do you see the mechanics I am attempting to explain here?

How do you become free of an impurity? You must begin by consciously seeing that you have the impurity. The moment you see that you have the impurity, you still have it; you are not free of it yet. When you see that you have any impurity, you will tend to react through the impurity of judging yourself. At the fourth level there is a certain pain that is inevitable. For that matter, there is a certain pain that is inevitable at every level of the path.

As we, who have been in embodiment on earth, all know, it is not pleasant to look at oneself and see that one has an impurity; one has some habit pattern that is self-destructive. It is never pleasant to see this. It is always a shock, but when you have experienced the unconditionality of love, you can begin to build a more constructive way to deal with this shock.

What is it that happens when you experience love as being unconditional? Which part of you, of your psyche, of your being, can experience unconditional love? Do you think the ego can experience unconditional love? Obviously not. Can the analytical mind experience unconditional love? No, because it wants to give it some sort of characteristic that it can use to analyze and catalogue it. Unconditional love is unconditional because it is beyond anything that can be defined on earth.

The only part of your being that can experience unconditional love is the Conscious You. The Conscious You can experience unconditional love only when it steps outside of the soul vehicle, your four lower bodies, the outer mind, the ego, whatever you want to call this conglomerate that is your vehicle for expressing yourself in the material world. When you step outside of this, even for a moment, *that* is when you experience unconditionality.

The Conscious You has no reaction

You can use this experience, once you have become consciously aware of having had it, to start looking at how you react when you are confronted with something in yourself that you need to see. You can begin to ask yourself: "What is it that is reacting this way? Is it the Conscious You that I really am, or is it some aspect of the outer soul vehicle, possibly the ego or an internal spirit or simply a habit pattern I have built up?" This is when you can begin to fathom one of the central reasons why we have given the teachings about the Conscious You. The stark reality, that can be extremely difficult to grasp at first, is that the Conscious You actually has no reaction to anything on earth.

You may have heard the story of Gautama Buddha sitting under the Bo tree in meditation, but before going into Nirvana, being confronted with the demons of Mara. The demons attempted to pull him into a reactionary pattern, but because he had attained complete clarity in knowing he was pure awareness and not any aspect of the outer mind, he could avoid reacting to the demons. There was no condition in him that could cause the conditional demons to pull him into a conditional reaction.

This can be very difficult to grasp at first. Even many ascended master students struggle with this—if they do not use the mechanism to outright reject the idea of the Conscious You. It is so easy to reject something when you do not like the ramifications of it. I can assure you that your ego does not like the idea that the core of your being reacts to nothing on earth. Why not? Because what is the ego's only way of capturing you? It is to get you to react.

You may think this sounds like a contradiction. The Conscious You has no reactions to anything on earth, but the ego can capture you by getting you to react. How is this possible? It is possible because the Conscious You does not react when it knows it is pure awareness, but the Conscious You can step into an internal spirit or a certain perception filter. Now, the Conscious You is experiencing the world through that filter, and the filter is reacting. When the Conscious You has forgotten that it is pure awareness and identifies itself with the filter, then the Conscious You *experiences* that it is reacting.

How do you become the Buddha? By beginning to become aware that, although there is an outer mechanism in your psyche that is reacting to the world, that mechanism is not *you*. You are more than this. As you purify your Conscious You from all illusions of Maya – the illusions that you are this, that or the next thing here on earth – then you can become aware that you are pure awareness. When you know you are pure awareness, you know you do not have to react to anything on earth.

In fact, *you* are not reacting. You become the open door where you are experiencing a condition on earth, but you are not reacting to it. You are letting the experience go right up to your I AM Presence. You allow your Presence to experience and process the condition, depositing a positive, life-supporting experience in your causal body. Do you see the essential difference?

When the Conscious You forgets who it is, it thinks it is an independent, separate being. The Conscious You then thinks that *it* is the one who has to react to everything in the world, who has to do something in the world, who has to accomplish something, who has a responsibility. You think that you are the doer, as Jesus taught so many years ago: "I can of my own self do nothing."

When the Conscious You thinks that it is the doer, it thinks that it is the one that has to process everything that happens on earth. *You* do not have to process anything that happens on earth. You experience it, and then you let the experience rise to your I AM Presence and let your I AM Presence process the experience. Then you wait. If there is an outer reaction to be done, you let it come from the Presence instead of deciding with some aspect of your outer mind what response should be forthcoming.

You do not have to react right now

One of the primary mechanisms used by the fallen beings, by your ego, and by other people in order to manipulate you is to get you into a situation where you feel: "Here is something I have to react to right now! There is no time to step outside of the outer self, to let the experience rise to my I AM Presence and to neutrally and calmly wait for a response from the Presence." They want you to believe that you do not have time. You have to react *right now.* "I want an answer right now. You need to take action right now."

Do you see how this is one of the dynamics in any love relationship? Many of you have experienced having partners who get upset or emotional and what is the worst thing you can do to them? It is to ignore them, to not react to them being upset. Then they get *really* upset. What do you do instead? You go into the outer self and now you react through the outer self.

My beloved, can you honestly look at your life and see that reacting to a situation through the outer self ever improved things? Did it not instead create a reaction in the other person that led to another reaction in you? Pretty soon, you had created a downward spiral where none of you could now react to each other with love. You were locked in reacting through your own psychological wounds, and none of you were able to pull yourself out of this and stop the tension, the argument or whatever pattern you were trapped in.

Your right to delay a reaction

You do have a right to delay a reaction to a given situation. I admit there are some situations where you need to take quick action. There are also many, many situations where you could say: "I'm sorry, but I need some time to process this situation and find a love-based reaction." Your partner may not like this at all, but you have a right to step aside and not react to the situation right now, especially when you feel an emotional reaction inside of you where you know you will just be repeating an old pattern.

Many relationships have been ruined by both people going into such a reactionary pattern, the spiral starting, and then, none of them can stop it. Once you are caught in this downward pull of reacting and feeling you have to react right now, there is no room for a love-based reaction. You are reacting through whatever patterns and internal spirits you have—both of you. If the spiral is going to be broken, then at least one person must step outside of the spiral, look at the situation from the outside and find a different reaction.

Again, this may not work. This may not change your partner, but then you still build a momentum that will cause you to flow on to a different situation. You will never get a bad result from a love-based reaction. You may not get a love-based response from your partner. In the short run, it may seem as if your partner only gets more upset the more loving you are. It is important for you to understand why this is so.

How dark spirits feed off the negative spiral

There is a measure you can apply to almost all relationships. When both partners are trapped in fear-based reactions, the spiral cannot be stopped. If one partner is able to step out of the spiral and find a love-based reaction, then the spiral has been challenged. If the other partner responds to this by becoming even more upset, then you know that this partner is trapped in an internal spirit that does not want that person to be free to have a love-based reaction.

If you are able to respond to your partner with love and your partner gets more upset with you, you know that there is an internal spirit, and possibly external spirits or demons, that are using your partner to try to get your energy. These dark spirits simply want the spiral to continue so that both of you feed your energy into it [For more information on these topics, see *Cosmology of Evil*].

A human being will always respond somewhat positively to love. Dark spirits, of course, will not. They will do what they have always done: attempt to put down love. When your partner is reacting to love with a fear-based response, you know that your partner is not reacting as a human being because your partner is trapped in one of these spirits. In most relationships, both partners are trapped in such spirits. They are reacting to each other through the spirits and that is why the spiral cannot be broken. If one person is able to step outside, and the other person still reacts by being upset, then you know that this person is temporarily taken over by dark spirits.

You can then make the calls for your partner to be cut free. If your partner is spiritual, you may be able to talk about this at times when your partner is not upset. You cannot apply force to your partner. You can give your partner time. You can make the calls. You can strive to always react with love—even when your partner gets upset. You can refuse to be bullied into the usual patterns, and then you can wait until, somehow, you get a signal from your I AM Presence that it is time to move on. Then you move on and you forgive.

Transcending the memory of the impurity

If you do not move on but stay in the relationship, then two partners can face the next challenge. Let us say that you become aware that you have been in a pattern in your relationship. You both make an effort to see what it is in yourself that causes you to react, and then you transcend that pattern. Now, you face the next challenge of purity. Once you have acknowledged that you have an impurity, once you have looked at the impurity and actually seen the illusion that caused it, what do you then do to overcome the memory of having been in this impurity?

First, you must see the impurity. Then you must be willing to go into it and look at the illusion that caused you to respond with a fear-based reaction. Once you see that illusion and dissolve it, you are free from the matrix. You can then use our decrees and invocations to consume the energy that you misqualified. Once you have consumed the energy, you are technically free of the impurity, but not quite because you still have the memory.

Let us say that you have a relationship that is beginning to be more aware and mature. You have been able to talk about a certain pattern in your relationship. You have been able to help each other gain clarity over your reactions and you have risen above it. What do you now do about the fact that you remember that you used to have this problem and that your partner used to be *this* way, and that you used to be *that* way?

The challenge of purity, the challenge of the Fourth Ray, is not simply a matter of changing your attitude, behavior or beliefs or of purifying energies. It is a matter of purifying your mind entirely of even the memory. Forgiveness is important, but forgiveness is not complete until you have forgotten the wrong. This is the biggest challenge on the Fourth Ray: How do you erase a memory?

I am not here talking about relationships where there have been obvious forms of abuse. I am talking about most relationships where there is not physical violence, physical abuse, sexual abuse, or other forms of abusive behavior. In that case, it is more complicated, and it is beyond what I want to discourse on here. What I want to talk about is most relationships that get in a negative pattern. What do you do once you break the pattern? How do you get over the memory?

This is where unconditional love is essential. What is it that really happens when you experience unconditional love? You realize, or at least you begin to sense, that if God's love is unconditional, then no matter what you have done on earth, you can be free of it. This is something that many people find it difficult to accept. Even many ascended master students cannot quite accept this. The reason is that this planet is so heavily infused with the judgmentalness of the fallen beings.

The essence of the judgmental consciousness

What is the essence of the judgmental consciousness? It is to get you to feel that, because you have done this terrible wrong, you can *never* be redeemed, you can never again be pure. Why did Jesus say that only the man that descended from heaven can ascend back to heaven? Because the "man" who descended from heaven is the Conscious You and it is pure awareness. How can the Conscious You ascend back to the I AM Presence? Only by once again becoming pure awareness, not identifying itself with any of the conditions in the soul vehicle.

What the world, the demons of this world, want you to believe is that because the Conscious You has stepped into the outer self and seen the world through it, it can never again step out of it. What does this get you into? It gets you into the thinking created by the fallen beings that, in order to ascend back to heaven, you need to perfect the soul vehicle. You need to purify it of what the judgmental consciousness defines as impure so that you have only in your soul vehicle that which is defined as pure. So many people have been tricked by this—*so* many people.

Judging yourself and your partner

What does it get you into? It gets you into a state of mind where you are constantly judging, evaluating and analyzing yourself. Because you cannot stand this, what do most people do? They go into the consciousness described by Jesus when he talked about the beam in your own eye. You are not able to handle constantly judging yourself, but you cannot stop the judging consciousness so you deflect it away from yourself and direct it towards others. Who is the primary person that you direct it towards? It is your partner in a love relationship. There may be others as well, but certainly, your partner is the one who gets the brunt of it. You will all have experienced that, while you are in love, you are not doing this.

Do you see that being in love temporarily sets aside this tendency to judge? You think that now you have found the perfect partner who will complete you and make you feel good about yourself?. While this illusion lasts, you have no need to judge your partner. When the honeymoon is over, as they say, you go back into the old patterns. One day you realize that your partner does not live up to your idolatrous image, your partner will not complete you, will not make you feel good about yourself. Then you go back into the pattern of directing judgment away from yourself.

So many people are trapped in this pattern of feeling bad about themselves to the point where they cannot stand it. As a survival mechanism, they direct this feeling away from themselves, projecting that if only others had this or that fault, then it is not so bad that you are not perfect either. Step back and ask yourself: "Where does this feeling that I am bad, inadequate or unwhole come from?"

How can the Conscious You be unwhole or bad when it is pure awareness and has no conditions? Where does the idea that you are bad come from? It comes from the judgmental consciousness. It is not that your soul vehicle is bad or is a sinner. The idea that you are a sinner or a bad person comes only from the judgmental consciousness that is created by the fallen beings. You will always feel bad about yourself until you realize that what makes you feel bad is a certain state of consciousness that you have accepted into your soul vehicle. You are judging yourself through that consciousness and you will only be able to see things that make you feel bad.

You can go into what so many people on the spiritual path have done: Trying to purify yourself of all that is defined as "bad" according to your spiritual teaching. You can launch into a frantic effort to give enough decrees and invocations (and purify yourself and fast and do this and do that) until you feel that you live up to the conditions for what your teaching defines as pure. What you will discover after having done this is that, although you have made some progress, you are still feeling bad about yourself. The reason is that what makes you feel bad is not the impurities or the purities but the consciousness that judges based on a standard that defines relative impure and relative pure. You will stop feeling bad about yourself only when you make contact with the unconditional purity of God. Once you have experienced unconditional love, you can move on and realize that purity also has an unconditional aspect.

The ray of acceleration

This is why Serapis Bey has called the Fourth Ray the ray of acceleration. He wants to get away from using the word purity, which in most people's minds is locked to the opposite of impurity. Most people see it as dualistic. Serapis Bey does not see purity as a dualistic quality, for he has transcended duality in order to become an ascended master. Most people see it that way, and this is what you need to accelerate yourself beyond. You can then find a way to apply unconditional love to accelerate your relationship out of the memory of the old hurt and the old patterns.

I will admit that very few relationships will make it to that point once they have gone into a downward spiral—very, very few. The reason is that there is such an imbalance between the sexes on earth. There is such a cloud of animosity and opposition created between men and women that it is so difficult to break through it.

If you have been in a relationship that entered a negative pattern and you were not able to break out of it, I am not asking you to feel bad about this. I am asking you to forgive yourself and realize you were up against very heavy odds on this planet. I am also giving this teaching because I hope that those who follow this course will be willing to apply the teaching and become better at taking relationships out of the pattern and even the memory. Hopefully, the tools that we give you in this course will help you be successful in your personal life and in your relationships. This is always our aim.

By me pointing out an impurity, do not use my teaching to feel bad about yourself or to give up. Do not feel like you can never be redeemed because you look at your life and see how you have been trapped in that pattern. Instead, use my teaching to recognize how difficult it is to maintain a loving relationship on earth. Then decide that now that you *know* better, you will *do* better from now on.

Becoming pure after seeing an impurity

How do you become pure once you become aware that you have been impure? *You cannot!* I said that all of the dark forces in this universe want you to believe that once you have done something that is impure, you can never be redeemed. I am now going to tell you something that might shock you: They are actually right.

They are right only in the sense that the "you" who did the impure thing is not the "Conscious You." It is an unreal "you" created in the soul vehicle in the form of an internal spirit. That "you" can never be purified. You can never feel pure as long as you are looking at life from inside that spirit. What does it take for you to become free of the spirit? Here is another subtlety.

Many ascended master students take our teachings, and they are awakened to the fact that they have had some impurity in their being. They naturally want to be free of it and now they think: "I have to purify my mind, my soul, of this." Again, there is a truth here. In your four lower bodies, there is a certain amount of misqualified energy that has been generated through the impure self. This you have to purify by invoking light, directing it into the impure energy and raising its vibration. The impure self, you do not have to purify and you *cannot* purify. As long as you are seeking to purify the impure self in order to make it acceptable to God, then you are only tying yourself to the impure self.

What you *need* to do is to see the illusion that created the impure self. Once you see that it is an illusion, you will naturally see that it is unreal. Then you can consciously step outside of it by focusing on the fact that you are the Conscious You and you are pure awareness. Whatever you may have gone into was only a perception filter. It caused you to *see* the world as impure or *see* yourself as impure, but you had not *become* impure.

When you put on your sunglasses and go outside, the sun looks different. Did the fact that you, on planet earth, put on a pair of sunglasses change the sun, which is thousands upon thousands of miles away? Of course it didn't. Did the fact that your Conscious You put on the glasses of an impure self change your I AM Presence? Nay. Did the fact that you put on sunglasses change *you,* or did it only change the way you look at the world? Did the fact that the Conscious You put on an impure self change the Conscious You?

All of the demons of this world will say: "Yes, it did! You were changed by the fact that you took on this impure self and you went into this world. Just look at what you have done! Look how terrible the consequences were! Of course, you were changed by this! You can't just turn around and walk away and run away from this. What this master is telling you is a lie! He is just telling you to deny that you have done something in the past!"

I am not telling you to deny what you did in the past. I am telling you to look at it openly and honestly. What the demons are telling you is that you do not have to look at what you have done in the past because there is some outer way whereby you can purify yourself and be redeemed: "Jesus will come and take away your impure self. You do not have to look at it." Or Krishna, or the Buddha, or the violet flame, or this or that will do it for you.

Jesus told you to look at the beam in your own eye. Once you see it, you also see that it was an unreal self and not the Conscious You. That is when you, as the *conscious* You, can say: "But you know, I have done my job here. I have purified the energies I misqualified through that impure self. I have seen the illusion. Because I have done my job, I *can* walk away from this. I do not have to purify this imperfect self. I do not have to make it acceptable in the eyes of God because it never will be. You, demons of Mara, have nothing in me. I don't need to react to you. I can simply walk away from you, for the Prince of this world has nothing in me, at least not at this particular point, for I am back to the purity with which I descended. I have become as the little child, as the pure, innocent self that descended."

When you can reach that stage, one of two things will happen in your relationship: Either your partner will respond and also be transformed, and you can start building a positive spiral, or your partner will refuse to be changed, and then you will flow on in your life. When you have become innocent, you cannot remain in a relationship with a person who continues to put down the innocent. It just isn't possible. Innocence is its own reward because it is the gateway to infinite joy.

Clearing the memory of the impurity

At my retreat, we can show you graphically, visually on a screen the impurities in your being. The lower part of your aura, your personal energy field, forms what we sometimes call the electronic belt. All of the fear-based energies that you generate gravitate here. For most people, there is quite a lot of turbulence in this electronic belt. If you were to be shown this all at once, it might be overwhelming to you. What we do at my retreat is to show you a little bit, and then we show you how to focus on that task, invoke the light to clear out the energies, then go into that internal spirit, that unreal self, and see the illusion behind it. Then we show you how to let go of the self itself and the feeling that you are that self and that you are tied to it forever.

We show that the akashic records can be cleared, and therefore, God no longer remembers the impurity. If God does not remember it, why would *you* want to remember it? This also brings up the question: "If you have purified yourself of your reaction to your partner and what your partner did to you in the past, why would you want to remember what your partner did?" I know that the outer mind will say: "What if my partner has not freed himself or herself from that pattern? What if my partner still has that same tendency and still does that thing?"

Your partner may not have risen above the pattern, but when you have purified yourself of the need to react to your partner, then the last step is to simply let go of the memory of what your partner did so that each day you meet your partner on a clean white slate. Your partner may abuse you again, but if you do not react because you have freed yourself from the reactionary pattern, then you just forget it again and you meet each day on a blank sheet. When you can do this, you can come to that point of simply flowing away from a partner that will not change.

Leaving a relationship or flowing on

I know that many of you have found it very difficult to leave a relationship. I have cautioned you against deciding with the outer mind to leave. That is why I am giving you more teaching on how to purify yourself and your reactions to your partner as long as you are in the relationship. The more pure you can become, the easier for you it will be to come to that point where you are not actually making a decision to leave. You are just seeing that this is the next logical step.

Many of you have made the decision to leave a relationship, but because you had not quite purified yourself of your reactionary patterns, it was very difficult to make that decision. You were agonizing over it: "Was it the right decision or wasn't it? Was there more I could have done? Was there more I *should* have done?" In many cases, it *was* the right decision to leave, but maybe it was a little too early to leave because you had not quite purified yourself of the reactionary patterns. That is why I am cautioning you that if you will make an effort to work on overcoming your own reactionary patterns, then you will come to that point where it is not a matter of agonizing over a decision. You just see that it is the next natural stage on your personal path to flow out of this relationship, and then you can do so with a greater sense of peace.

How the death consciousness affects relationships

There is an aspect of the judgmental consciousness of the fallen beings that is directed at relationships and that sets people up so that their relationships are almost doomed to failure. The goal of the fallen beings is not necessarily to get a relationship to break up. The goal of the fallen beings is to put you down no matter what happens.

They do not care if you stay in a relationship for a lifetime and go into a limiting pattern where you are limiting yourself and your partner, or whether you break out of the relationship and then go into a pattern of condemning yourself or doubting whether it was the right thing to do. As long as they can put you down or make you feel inadequate or impure, the fallen beings are—well, not really happy because they never will be. But they are at least feeling like they are having power and that they are proving their point that God was wrong for giving you free will.

In many cultures, there has for a very long time been this consciousness that a relationship should be for life: "Till death do us part." What is death? Is it physical death or is it the death consciousness? Many people have lived together physically for a lifetime, but death parted them long ago because they both went into a pattern where none of them were growing. This is the death consciousness, and it did part you even if you are physically together.

The real goal of the ascended masters is growth. Have you not at this point realized that we of the ascended masters do not consider the earth an ideal planet? It is a very low planet. The purpose of embodying here is *not* to experience some edenic state on earth because this is not currently possible, given the collective consciousness. What *is* the purpose of embodying here for a spiritual person? It is to raise your own consciousness and thereby raise the collective. You are here to have the maximum possible growth from being here and then get out of here as quickly as possible by ascending.

The spiritual purpose of relationships

What is the purpose of a relationship? It is to have the maximum possible growth and then move on. It doesn't mean you have to move on physically, but it means that when a man and a woman come together, then they have something in their psychology that they are meant to help each other work out. What is the real purpose of a relationship? It is not that you make each other feel good. It is not that you live happily ever after.

Why were you attracted to each other? It is because your partner has something in his or her psychology that will cause you to react. Your reaction will make visible what you have of unresolved psychology in yourself. Your partner is the one who is best suited for making visible what you cannot see in yourself. When two people come together, the higher purpose for the relationship is that they both make visible in the other what they cannot see. Once they have made the major thing that attracted them visible, then the relationship has fulfilled its first purpose. The highest outcome is, of course, that the partners can help each other overcome the tendency as well.

In many cases, what happens is that the two partners make visible in each other what they don't want to see or are not able to see. They are so shocked by this that the honeymoon ends abruptly, and in some cases, the marriage ends very quickly. This does not necessarily mean the relationship has failed. The two people can still process the experience afterwards—if they are willing. They can learn the lesson and move on. Even a relationship that lasted for less than a year can have been successful in fulfilling its first purpose.

If the partners can grow from their first shocking encounter, then they can go on to the next challenge. Then perhaps they can go on to the next, and therefore, you can build a lifelong relationship.

In this day and age, if you are a spiritual person dedicated to maximum spiritual growth in this lifetime, possibly qualifying for your ascension in this lifetime, it is very unlikely that you will be with the same partner for all of your life. In most cases, maximum growth requires several partners. That is just the nature of how intense the energies are on earth. Maximum growth on this planet requires you to move on to different situations in order to work out what you need to work out.

We of the ascended masters never consider a relationship a failure. We always consider it an *opportunity*. You may say: "But my relationship ended in a big argument, and we never learned our lessons." I would say: "You have not learned your lessons *yet*. If *you* are willing to ask for my guidance, I can help you learn *your* lesson. Then it doesn't matter to you whether your partner learns his or her lesson. You are only responsible for your own ascension, not that of your ex-partner."

Any relationship is simply an opportunity. You may not have grasped the opportunity, but that does not mean you have lost it. You just have not taken it yet, but you can take it at any time. Even twenty years after a relationship has ended, you can take the opportunity.

I will help you overcome any impurity

How can I say this? Because if you did not take the opportunity the first time it was presented, you obviously have not resolved the psychology. This means you still have that unresolved psychology in your being. You will be able to go back and look at the situation and remember it and say: "Oh, now I am beginning to see what I couldn't see back then. Let me get over this so that I do not drag this around with me. I have had enough of dragging this weight behind me as I am climbing the mountain of self. Why on earth have I carried this weight for so long? Why would I want to carry it one second longer when Paul the Venetian is standing right there with his big smile saying: 'Just ask and I will help you!' I am going to take his hand. I am going to take him up on this offer. I am going to say: 'Paul, just help me get rid of this stuff! I have so had enough of it!'"

You see, my beloved, I know that you are pure, that the Conscious You is pure. I am willing to help you overcome absolutely any impurity in your being. Love is the great purifier.

You will not overcome all impurities as long as you are in my retreat, for the path goes on through the retreats of the other Chohans. While you are here, I will do my utmost to help you overcome as much as at all possible so that you are even better prepared to meet the other Chohans.

I see no impurity as real, but I do see *you* as real. I certainly know that *I* AM Real. *I AM* the Chohan of the Third Ray.

11 | I INVOKE LOVE TO CONSUME JUDGMENT

In the name I AM THAT I AM, Jesus Christ, I call to my I AM Presence to flow through the I Will Be Presence that I AM and give this invocation with full power. I call to beloved Elohim Heros and Amora and Purity and Astrea, Archangel Chamuel and Charity and Gabriel and Hope, Paul the Venetian and Serapis Bey to help us transcend the tendency to blame each other or to keep each other from growing. Help us see and surrender all patterns that block our oneness with Paul the Venetian and with our I AM Presences, including …

[Make personal calls]

1. We are more than the outer selves

1. Paul the Venetian, help us experience unconditional love and accept that we are loved unconditionally.

O Heros-Amora, in your love so pink,
I care not what others about me may think,
in oneness with you, I claim a new day,
an innocent child, I frolic and play.

O Heros-Amora, a new life begun,
I laugh at the devil, the serious one,
I bathe in your glorious Ruby-Pink Sun,
knowing my God allows life to be fun.

2. Paul the Venetian, help us avoid feeling that because we have impurities, we could never be redeemed. Help us know that whatever impurities we discover, we could never lose God's unconditional love.

O Heros-Amora, life is such a joy,
I see that the world is like a great toy,
whatever my mind into it projects,
the mirror of life exactly reflects.

O Heros-Amora, I reap what I sow,
yet this is Plan B for helping me grow,
for truly, Plan A is that I join the flow,
immersed in the Infinite Love you bestow.

3. Paul the Venetian, help us know that the impurities we discover can only be conditions in the material world. No condition in the material world can make us unworthy of receiving the love that is beyond conditions.

O Heros-Amora, conditions you burn,
I know I AM free to take a new turn,
Immersed in the stream of infinite Love,
I know that my Spirit came from Above.

O Heros-Amora, awakened I see,
in true love is no conditionality,
the devil is stuck in his duality,
but I AM set free by Love's reality.

4. Paul the Venetian, help us transcend the tendency to condemn ourselves and each other through the judgmental consciousness of the fallen beings.

O Heros-Amora, I feel that at last,
I've risen above the trap of my past,
in true love I claim my freedom to grow,
forever I'm one with Love's Infinite Flow.

O Heros-Amora, conditions are ties,
forming a net of serpentine lies,
your love has no bounds, forever it flies,
raising all life into Ruby-Pink skies.

5. Paul the Venetian, help us step outside the soul vehicle and experience unconditional love. Help us use this experience to start looking at how we react to each other.

Beloved Astrea, your heart is so true,
your Circle and Sword of white and blue,
cut all life free from dramas unwise,
on wings of Purity our planet will rise.

Beloved Astrea, in God Purity,
accelerate all of my life energy,
raising my mind into true unity
with the Masters of love in Infinity.

6. Paul the Venetian, help us grasp and experience that the Conscious You has no reaction to anything on earth. It is only the ego that is reacting.

Beloved Astrea, from Purity's Ray,
send forth deliverance to all life today,
acceleration to Purity, I AM now free
from all that is less than love's Purity.

Beloved Astrea, in oneness with you,
your circle and sword of electric blue,
with Purity's Light cutting right through,
raising within me all that is true.

7. Paul the Venetian, help us grasp that when the Conscious You steps into an internal spirit or a perception filter, then we are experiencing that we are reacting. Yet this is only a perception.

Beloved Astrea, accelerate us all,
as for your deliverance I fervently call,
set all life free from vision impure
beyond fear and doubt, I AM rising for sure.

Beloved Astrea, I AM willing to see,
all of the lies that keep me unfree,
I AM rising beyond every impurity,
with Purity's Light forever in me.

8. Paul the Venetian, help us become aware that when we are reacting to each other with less than love, it is not our conscious selves but our egos that are reacting. Help us see that both of us are more than the ego.

Beloved Astrea, accelerate life
beyond all duality's struggle and strife,
consume all division between God and man,
accelerate fulfillment of God's perfect plan.

Beloved Astrea, I lovingly call,
break down separation's invisible wall,
I surrender all lies causing the fall,
forever affirming the oneness of All.

9\. Paul the Venetian, help us become the open door where we can experience a condition on earth but we are not reacting to it. We are allowing the I AM Presence to process the experience.

Accelerate into Oneness, I AM real,
Accelerate into Oneness, all life heal,
Accelerate into Oneness, I AM MORE,
Accelerate into Oneness, all will soar.

Accelerate into Oneness! (3X)
Beloved Heros and Amora.
Accelerate into Oneness! (3X)
Beloved Chamuel and Charity.
Accelerate into Oneness! (3X)
Beloved Paul the Venetian.
Accelerate into Oneness! (3X)
Beloved I AM.

2. We do not have to react through the ego

1. Paul the Venetian, help us overcome the illusion that we have to react to everything in the world, that we have to do something in the world, that we have to accomplish something, that we are the doers.

Chamuel Archangel, in ruby ray power,
I know I am taking a life-giving shower.
Love burning away all perversions of will,
I suddenly feel my desires falling still.

Chamuel Archangel, descend from Above,
Chamuel Archangel, with ruby-pink love,
Chamuel Archangel, so often thought-of,
Chamuel Archangel, o come Holy Dove.

2. Paul the Venetian, help us avoid the trap of thinking there is something we have to react to right now. Help us always take the time to let the I AM Presence decide the response.

Chamuel Archangel, a spiral of light,
as ruby ray fire now pierces the night.
All forces of darkness consumed by your fire,
consuming all those who will not rise higher.

Chamuel Archangel, descend from Above,
Chamuel Archangel, with ruby-pink love,
Chamuel Archangel, so often thought-of,
Chamuel Archangel, o come Holy Dove.

3. Paul the Venetian, help us break any pattern of reacting to each other through the outer self, trying to avoid that the other person becomes upset.

Chamuel Archangel, your love so immense,
with clarified vision, my life now makes sense.
The purpose of life you so clearly reveal,
immersed in your love, God's oneness I feel.

Chamuel Archangel, descend from Above,
Chamuel Archangel, with ruby-pink love,
Chamuel Archangel, so often thought-of,
Chamuel Archangel, o come Holy Dove.

4. Paul the Venetian, help us break the pattern of reacting to each other through our psychological wounds. Help us stop the tension, the argument and the reactionary pattern we are trapped in.

Chamuel Archangel, what calmness you bring,
I see now that even death has no sting.
For truly, in love there can be no decay,
as love is transcendence into a new day.

Chamuel Archangel, descend from Above,
Chamuel Archangel, with ruby-pink love,
Chamuel Archangel, so often thought-of,
Chamuel Archangel, o come Holy Dove.

5. Paul the Venetian, help us react to each other with a love-based response. Help us know that if this makes the partner more upset, then dark forces are using that partner to take away our harmony.

Gabriel Archangel, your light I revere,
immersed in your Presence, nothing I fear.
A disciple of Christ, I do leave behind,
the ego's desire for responding in kind.

Gabriel Archangel, of this I am sure,
Gabriel Archangel, Christ light is the cure.
Gabriel Archangel, intentions so pure,
Gabriel Archangel, in you I'm secure.

6. Paul the Venetian, help us be cut free from all internal and external spirits so we do not put down or reject the love from each other.

Gabriel Archangel, I fear not the light,
in purifications' fire, I delight.
With your hand in mine, each challenge I face,
I follow the spiral to infinite grace.

Gabriel Archangel, of this I am sure,
Gabriel Archangel, Christ light is the cure.
Gabriel Archangel, intentions so pure,
Gabriel Archangel, in you I'm secure.

7. Paul the Venetian, help us gain clarity over our reactions so we can overcome the pattern that is holding us back. Help us purify our minds from the memory of our past pattern.

Gabriel Archangel, your fire burning white,
ascending with you, out of the night.
My ego has nowhere to run and to hide,
in ascension's bright spiral, with you I abide.

Gabriel Archangel, of this I am sure,
Gabriel Archangel, Christ light is the cure.
Gabriel Archangel, intentions so pure,
Gabriel Archangel, in you I'm secure.

8. Paul the Venetian, help us accept that because God's love is unconditional, no matter what we have done on earth, we can be free of it.

Gabriel Archangel, your trumpet I hear,
announcing the birth of Christ drawing near.
In lightness of being, I now am reborn,
rising with Christ on bright Easter morn.

Gabriel Archangel, of this I am sure,
Gabriel Archangel, Christ light is the cure.
Gabriel Archangel, intentions so pure,
Gabriel Archangel, in you I'm secure.

9. Paul the Venetian, help us see and escape the pattern where none of us can stand judging ourselves, and therefore we start judging our partner instead.

With angels I soar,
as I reach for MORE.
The angels so real,
their love all will heal.
The angels bring peace,
all conflicts will cease.
With angels of light,
we soar to new height.

The rustling sound of angel wings,
what joy as even matter sings,
what joy as every atom rings,
in harmony with angel wings.

3. We do not have to condemn each other

1. Paul the Venetian, help us see that the tendency to judge ourselves comes from the judgmental consciousness created by the fallen beings.

Master Paul, venetian dream,
your love for beauty's flowing stream.
Master Paul, in love's own womb,
your power shatters ego's tomb.

O Holy Spirit, flow through me,
I am the open door for thee.
O mighty rushing stream of Light,
transcendence is my sacred right.

2. Paul the Venetian, help us stop feeling bad about ourselves by making contact with the unconditional purity of God. Help us accelerate our relationship out of the memory of the old hurt.

Master Paul, your counsel wise,
my mind is raised to lofty skies.
Master Paul, in wisdom's love,
such beauty flowing from Above.

O Holy Spirit, flow through me,
I am the open door for thee.
O mighty rushing stream of Light,
transcendence is my sacred right.

3. Paul the Venetian, help us break through the collective cloud of animosity and opposition between men and women. Help us find a love-based way of relating to each other.

Master Paul, love is an art,
it opens up the secret heart.
Master Paul, love's rushing flow,
my heart awash in sacred glow.

O Holy Spirit, flow through me,
I am the open door for thee.
O mighty rushing stream of Light,
transcendence is my sacred right.

4. Paul the Venetian, help us see the internal spirit that we have created in our relationship. Help us see that we are both more than this spirit. Help us allow both ourselves and each other to leave behind that spirit.

Master Paul, accelerate,
upon pure love I meditate.
Master Paul, intentions pure,
my self-transcendence will ensure.

O Holy Spirit, flow through me,
I am the open door for thee.
O mighty rushing stream of Light,
transcendence is my sacred right.

5. Paul the Venetian, help us overcome the planetary momentum that causes people to blame each other and be unwilling to let go of the past. Help us set each other free to have a harmonious relationship or move on with our lives.

Master Paul, your love will heal,
my inner light you do reveal.
Master Paul, all life console,
with you I'm being truly whole.

O Holy Spirit, flow through me,
I am the open door for thee.
O mighty rushing stream of Light,
transcendence is my sacred right.

6. Paul the Venetian, help us free ourselves from the tendency to react to each other through the outer self. Help us let go of the memory of what happened in the past so that each day we meet each other on a clean white slate.

Master Paul, you serve the All,
by helping us transcend the fall.
Master Paul, in peace we rise,
as ego meets its sure demise.

O Holy Spirit, flow through me,
I am the open door for thee.
O mighty rushing stream of Light,
transcendence is my sacred right.

7. Paul the Venetian, help us see how to raise our relationship to a higher level or help us see if moving on separately is the next logical step.

Master Paul, love all life free,
your love is for eternity.
Master Paul, you are the One,
to help us make the journey fun.

O Holy Spirit, flow through me,
I am the open door for thee.
O mighty rushing stream of Light,
transcendence is my sacred right.

8. Paul the Venetian, help us focus on overcoming our reactionary patterns. Help us come to the point where we can flow to a higher stage or flow out of the relationship with a sense of peace.

Master Paul, you balance all,
the seven rays upon my call.
Master Paul, you paint the sky,
with colors that delight the I.

O Holy Spirit, flow through me,
I am the open door for thee.
O mighty rushing stream of Light,
transcendence is my sacred right.

9. Paul the Venetian, help us see that the goal of the fallen beings is to put us down whether we stay in a limited relationship or separate in a state of disharmony.

Master Paul, your Presence here,
filling up my inner sphere.
Life is now a sacred flow,
God Love I do on all bestow.

O Holy Spirit, flow through me,
I am the open door for thee.
O mighty rushing stream of Light,
transcendence is my sacred right.

4. We are helping each other grow

1. Paul the Venetian, help us overcome the collective pattern that a relationship should last for life. Help us accept that growth is the most important aspect of our lives.

Serapis Bey, what power lies,
behind your purifying eyes.
Serapis Bey, it is a treat,
to enter your sublime retreat.

O Holy Spirit, flow through me,
I am the open door for thee.
O mighty rushing stream of Light,
transcendence is my sacred right.

2. Paul the Venetian, help us see that the purpose of embodying on earth is to raise our own consciousness and thereby raise the collective. The purpose of a relationship is to have the maximum possible growth.

Serapis Bey, what wisdom found,
your words are always most profound.
Serapis Bey, I tell you true,
my mind has room for naught but you.

O Holy Spirit, flow through me,
I am the open door for thee.
O mighty rushing stream of Light,
transcendence is my sacred right.

3. Paul the Venetian, help us see that when a man and a woman come together, they have something in their psychology that they are meant to help each other work out.

Serapis Bey, what love beyond,
my heart does leap, as I respond.
Serapis Bey, your life a poem,
that calls me to my starry home.

O Holy Spirit, flow through me,
I am the open door for thee.
O mighty rushing stream of Light,
transcendence is my sacred right.

4. Paul the Venetian, help us accept that the real purpose of our relationship is not to live happily ever after but to help each other heal our unresolved psychology.

Serapis Bey, your guidance sure,
my base is clear and white and pure.
Serapis Bey, no longer trapped,
by soul in which my self was wrapped.

O Holy Spirit, flow through me,
I am the open door for thee.
O mighty rushing stream of Light,
transcendence is my sacred right.

5. Paul the Venetian, help us accept that the higher purpose of our relationship is that we make visible in each other what we cannot see so we can rise above those patterns.

Serapis Bey, what healing balm,
in mind that is forever calm.
Serapis Bey, my thoughts are pure,
your discipline I shall endure.

O Holy Spirit, flow through me,
I am the open door for thee.
O mighty rushing stream of Light,
transcendence is my sacred right.

6. Paul the Venetian, help us avoid going into a negative reaction where we blame each other for doing exactly what we are meant to do, even thinking our relationship has failed.

Serapis Bey, what secret test,
for egos who want to be best.
Serapis Bey, expose in me,
all that is less than harmony.

O Holy Spirit, flow through me,
I am the open door for thee.
O mighty rushing stream of Light,
transcendence is my sacred right.

7. Paul the Venetian, help us rise above our old pattern of being shocked at each others differences. Help us build a lasting relationship of helping each other grow spiritually.

Serapis Bey, what moving sight,
my self ascends to sacred height.
Serapis Bey, forever free,
in sacred synchronicity.

O Holy Spirit, flow through me,
I am the open door for thee.
O mighty rushing stream of Light,
transcendence is my sacred right.

8. Paul the Venetian, help us accept that the ascended masters never consider a relationship a failure but always consider it an opportunity. Help us see the opportunity in our relationship even if we are no longer in a physical relationship.

Serapis Bey, you balance all,
the seven rays upon my call.
Serapis Bey, in space and time,
the pyramid of self, I climb.

O Holy Spirit, flow through me,
I am the open door for thee.
O mighty rushing stream of Light,
transcendence is my sacred right.

9. Paul the Venetian, help us see that even if our relationship has ended at the physical level, we still have the opportunity to process the experience and grow from it. Help us reconnect to our desire for growth and help each other make maximum progress towards our ascensions.

Serapis Bey, your Presence here,
filling up my inner sphere.
Life is now a sacred flow,
God Purity I do bestow.

O Holy Spirit, flow through me,
I am the open door for thee.
O mighty rushing stream of Light,
transcendence is my sacred right.

Sealing:

In the name of the Divine Mother, I fully accept that the power of these calls is used to set free the Ma-ter light, so it can outpicture the perfect vision of Christ for my own life, for all people and for the planet. In the name I AM THAT I AM, it is done! Amen.

12 | LOVE AND TRUTH

I AM Paul the Venetian. What happens when you reach the fifth level at my retreat? This is where you face the combination of love with the Fifth Ray, which has often been called the ray of truth. "What is truth?" as Pontius Pilate asked Jesus. This is worth contemplating.

Reality and your perception of reality

Pontius Pilate represented a person who was below the 48th level of consciousness. Jesus represented a person who was very close to the 144th level of consciousness. As you get close to that 144th level, you can know truth. While you are below the 48th level, you will never know truth. When you come to my retreat, you are not below the 48th but neither are you close to the 144th.

Can you know truth at the level you are at when you come to my retreat? You can know a higher expression of truth than while you are below the 48th level. You cannot know the fullness of truth that you can know when you get close to the 144th. This is very important to keep in mind. What is it you *can* know? How can you see truth when you are somewhere between the 48th and the 96th level on the path of self-mastery?

You can see truth only through the soul vehicle that you are using as an expression in the material world. This does not mean you cannot experience truth in its pure sense. The Conscious You has the ability to step outside of its identification with the soul vehicle. As you can experience unconditional love, you can experience unconditional truth, but unconditional truth is unconditional. It has no conditions.

We need to make a subtle distinction that the vast majority of the people on this planet do not even understand. They see no need to make this distinction because they see no difference between reality and their perception of reality. They think that what they see through the soul vehicle is reality, is truth, but it is not, is it? You have begun to rise above the 48th level and you have started to disassociate yourself, disidentify yourself, from that soul vehicle.

Your soul vehicle is not your enemy

Here is the distinction you need to make: The soul vehicle is not an enemy of your spiritual growth. It *can* be, and it certainly *is* below the 48th level. When you are below the 48th level, the soul vehicle, which includes the ego, will pull you into self-centered patterns, fear-based patterns. You are seeking to defend the ego and the lower self instead of being willing to rise above the ego and the more selfish aspects of the human consciousness.

The human consciousness and the ego give a colored overlay to the soul vehicle. When you rise above the 48th level, you have begun to escape this self-centeredness. As you rise higher on the path of self-mastery towards the 96th level, you shed more and more of it. This does not mean that at this point you shed the soul vehicle.

The purpose of the path of self-mastery between the 48th and the 96th level is to help you develop your creative abilities so that you can express them better in the physical realm. When you express your creative abilities, you have to express them through some vehicle. You have to have four lower bodies. That is why the Conscious You, in its state of pure awareness, cannot express any creativity. That is why the Conscious You needs to create the soul vehicle, including the four lower bodies. It does not need to create the ego, but it has done so on a dense planet like earth. The main task on the path of self-mastery is to rise above the influence of the ego so that you have mastery over the soul vehicle instead of having the ego being the master of the soul vehicle and pulling you into repeating these fear-based patterns that end up defending the ego.

How the soul vehicle has been developed

I have earlier talked about the need to stop purifying the internal spirits and give them up, but the internal spirits are not your soul vehicle in its pure form. The internal spirits are created based on the ego's fear and distorted perception. They are created based on an illusion, a dualistic illusion, but it is possible to have a soul vehicle that is purified of these. This still does not mean that the soul vehicle can ascend, but it does mean that you have a more pure vehicle through which you can express yourself in the material world.

How did you develop your particular soul vehicle? You did so based on the individuality built into, defined in, your I AM Presence. Your I AM Presence has a unique individual matrix that is different from that of any other self-aware being in the entire world of form. Even though you may not be conscious of your I AM Presence, you are still expressing the individuality of your I AM Presence to some degree when you are creating your soul vehicle.

Your soul vehicle is also created based on the experiences you have in the material world. If you have embodied on planet earth for a long time, which you have if you are ready to engage in this course, then your individuality, the individuality of your soul vehicle, has been influenced by what you have experienced on earth. This is just the way life is. It is the same for all of us when we are in embodiment.

The task between the 48th and the 96th level is to purify your soul vehicle of the ego, but not to get rid of the soul vehicle or to take all individuality away from the soul vehicle. This is something you do after the 96th level where you begin to free the Conscious You from even the non-fear-based aspects of your soul vehicle.

We might say that you first build a soul vehicle that is pure so that you have a vehicle through which you can express yourself, but then you start disidentifying yourself from the soul vehicle so that you realize that you are – you *are* – the Presence, an extension of the Presence. The vehicle is just that: A vehicle that your creativity flows through in the material realm. You could say that above the 96th level, you are dismantling the individuality or the soul vehicle that you had built up until the 96th level, but this is not entirely what happens. You are not ending up having no personality at the 144th level.

You will see that Jesus had a distinct personality. It is not described very accurately in the Scriptures, but he did have a certain personality. There was nothing wrong with this because he was not identified with it. Other people might look at this and say that the Christ in embodiment could not possibly have such a personality and use that as an excuse for rejecting him. Some people who met him back then did exactly that, but that was *their* choice and not Jesus' responsibility. You might have aspects of a certain human personality with you until you ascend, but it is not consequential for your ascension. It is just a vehicle.

Why am I telling you this? Because it relates to the initiations you face at the fifth level of my retreat. One of the perversions of love that you have to deal with at my retreat is precisely this tendency to think that truth can be only one way. If you really love somebody and want to help them and set them free, you *must* make them see the truth.

My beloved, if you are standing, looking at the sun setting in the West and you are facing the sun, then you are having a certain perspective. If you now turn around and look the other way, you are not seeing the sun, are you? When you, as the Conscious You, go within and withdraw from the soul vehicle, you can look up and see your I AM Presence. You may experience the unconditionality of truth, but you will also experience that unconditional truth is not expressed in words, not even in images, theories or philosophies.

What happens when you turn around and now you are looking *out* through your soul vehicle at the material world? You are now looking at the world *through* your soul vehicle and the individuality that is built into that vehicle. You can look at the concept of truth through that vehicle, but what I desire you to contemplate here is that you can never actually see absolute or unconditional truth through your soul vehicle.

This is precisely the perversion of love where the desire for something more gets perverted by the fallen consciousness into the desire for something ultimate. You have a natural desire for truth, but it gets perverted into the desire for an absolute truth that can be grasped by the soul vehicle.

A higher truth is not "the truth"

This is where you set the stage for a very large amount of the relationship problems you see on earth, not only in love relationships but in all kinds of human relationships. People believe that what they see through the soul vehicle is truth in some higher or even ultimate sense. In many cases, they believe that a particular religion or philosophical system has defined truth in its scriptures. If you accept that religion, you are seeing truth because you are accepting what that religion tells you about the world, even the spiritual world. This is not true because any religion that is expressed in the words and images of this world can only give you an approximation of truth. We have said this many times. The outer teaching, even the outer teachings we give, are meant to help you go beyond to the direct inner experience of the unconditional, that which cannot be expressed in, and certainly cannot be confined to, words and images.

Say we have two people. They both have a love for truth. They have a love for doing better. They recognize that what causes people to *not* do better is that they are caught in an illusion. They recognize that the way to overcome illusion is to see that it is an illusion, but here is where they become trapped in the subtleties of the fallen consciousness. The fallen consciousness says that in order to overcome a lie, you must see the truth. It is correct that in order to overcome a particular lie, you have to see that it is a lie. In order to see that a certain illusion is a lie, you need to see a higher expression of truth, but a higher expression of truth is not the same as "the truth" in an ultimate sense.

Overcoming the illusion of ultimate truth

The reason you got caught in a certain illusion was *not* that you were stupid. It was that you were at a certain level of consciousness. Through the perception filter at that level of consciousness, the illusion seemed true to you. When you accepted the illusion, it was because you saw it as truth.

You are not at the 144th level of consciousness, right? At your present level, you cannot see ultimate truth. Let us say that, at your present level of consciousness, you become aware that in a past life, when you were at a lower state of consciousness, you accepted a certain illusion. This illusion has been residing in your subconscious ever since then and it has affected you. It has become an internal spirit. You now see the fallacy of this internal spirit. You see that it is a dysfunctional pattern that you want to get out of, and then you come to see the illusion.

Why are you able to see the illusion that seemed like the truth to you in the past? It is because you have risen to a higher level of consciousness. You can see that what in the past seemed like the truth was not the truth but an illusion. What you now need to avoid is to believe in the fallen beings, the false teachers and your ego when they whisper in your ear that what you can see now is the *ultimate* truth. Instead, you need the humility of recognizing that what you see now is an expression of what you can see at your present level of consciousness, but because you are still far below the 144th level, you are not even close to seeing truth in its ultimate sense. What you *can* see now is an expression of your current level of consciousness, not some ultimate truth.

You now need to take the next step and realize that not only is what you see now an expression of your current level of consciousness, it is also an expression of your individuality, the individuality of your soul vehicle. As long as you are in embodiment, you will never actually see truth in an absolute sense. You will see it through your soul vehicle.

There are two aspects here. Underneath is the individuality of your soul vehicle, part of which you will carry with you until you ascend. Besides that, is the parallel track of what is your level of consciousness among the 144 possible. The closer you come to the 144th level, the more pure your perception will be, but it will still be an *individualized* perception.

The trap of having to persuade others

When you recognize this, you can avoid going into the trap that captures so many people. When you feel you love somebody, and when you desire to help them, and when you see that they are trapped in some kind of pattern, then you think the only way to help them is to make them see truth *as you see it*. Can you look at your own relationships and see if you have been in a situation where you believed that a certain person – be it a colleague, a boss, a parent, a child or a spouse – needed to see something that you could see in them but that they could not see in themselves? Did we not all experience this while we were in embodiment? Are you not all experiencing it now?

Now comes another subtle distinction. It may very well be that you *do* have a correct vision that the other person needs to overcome a certain pattern and that the other person is not seeing either the pattern or the illusion behind it. You may very well have the vision of this, and it may be correct that the other person needs to change. *However,* the other person will not change by coming to see the truth that you see.

Why is this so? Because the truth that you see is not ultimate truth and is an individualized truth. It is individualized for *you* based on the individuality of your soul vehicle and your present level of consciousness. What you see is not truth. You do not even see the situation with the other person and your relationship in an objective or clear manner. What you see is a *perception* produced by your soul vehicle. You are seeing through a glass darkly. You are seeing through colored glasses. *There is nothing wrong with this.* You can do nothing else at this point.

What I am pointing out to you is that the other person is not meant to see *your* perception because the other person has an individuality of his or her soul vehicle and also that person's current level of consciousness. The other person may be at a higher level of consciousness than you or may be at a lower level of consciousness. Even if the person is at a lower level of consciousness, it does not mean that the person will rise by seeing what you see. The person still needs to come to see it based on his or her soul vehicle and its present condition.

The ego's quest for universality

One of the universal perversions of the ego is that it does not recognize that it sees everything as an individualized perception. The ego desperately wants to make its individualized perception universal by getting all other people to accept it as "the truth." This is what I seek to help you begin to see and question when you come to the fifth level of my retreat. I attempt to help you recognize that what you see will always be individualized as long as you are in embodiment. What another person sees will also always be individualized while that person is in embodiment. The other person will not grow by coming to see things the way you see them. The person will grow by gaining a clearer perception based on its own individuality.

You rise by gaining a clearer perception, but your soul vehicle is still based on the individuality of your I AM Presence. Am I saying that your I AM Presence also has an individualized perception of the world? *Yes, it does.* You will have an individualized perception until you reach the Creator consciousness. Even beyond, you will be an individualized Creator. You will not have the kind of dualistic perception you have while you are in embodiment, while you are unascended, but it is still individualized. How could it be otherwise?

What makes me Paul the Venetian, as opposed to Hilarion? Or rather, not as *opposed to* but different from Hilarion? Hilarion and I are not the same. We certainly can blend and co-operate our energies while you are at the fifth level of my retreat, but we are not the same. We are not meant to become the same. It is not that, as we go further in our evolution, there will come a point where Hilarion and I have lost all individuality and we are now having no individuality. Do you think that Alpha and Omega have no individuality? Of course, not. You do not lose individuality. You raise it to higher and higher levels. This can be difficult to understand with the linear, analytical mind, I realize, but nevertheless, it is worth contemplating at this level.

Partners will never see anything exactly the same way

What I can do at my retreat is to show you how your soul vehicle affects your vision of anything that happens on earth. Your Conscious You can step outside of the perception filter of the soul vehicle. You can then experience a higher reality, but once you look at the world, looking away from your I AM Presence, you are seeing through the perception filter of the soul vehicle.

Your spouse in a love relationship will never – *ever* – come to see life exactly the way you see it. This is one of the most common causes for conflict in love relationships. You think, because you have been brought up to think this, that you are attracted to this partner because your partner is so like you. In reality, you were attracted to that partner because your partner can help you see something in yourself by making it visible. How does your partner make it visible? By getting you to *react to* your partner, not by getting you to see things the way your partner sees them.

I realize that this does not work very well in most relationships. Most people do not have the concept that they need to look at their reaction to their partner in order to discover their own unresolved psychology. Instead, they think that, in an ideal relationship, both you and your spouse should look at things exactly the same way. This will never happen. Even if it *could* happen, it would not give you growth.

What happens when I come together with Hilarion? What happens is that I realize he does not look at an issue the same way I look at it. Because I am an ascended master, I do not see that as a threat. I realize that he has a different perspective, and perhaps that can help me gain a different perspective on a particular issue so I can see a broader way to deal with it. That is the strength of being different. When I see that Hilarion perceives a situation differently, it expands my sense of self. His is expanded by experiencing how I perceive the situation.

This is the way it ideally *should* be in love relationships on earth. How *can* it be when you have been programmed with this dysfunctional belief that, in order to have a harmonious relationship, you should look at things in exactly the same way? What you need in order to have a harmonious relationship is the recognition that your perception is an individualized perception and that your partner should not come to see things the way you see them by accepting your perception. Your partner should expand his or her individualized vision, but it should be allowed to be individualized.

If both of you can accept this and can allow each other to grow in your own ways, then you can have a harmonious relationship that still provides growth. If just one partner cannot see this, but continues to insist on getting the other person to see it "my way," then you cannot have a harmonious relationship. It is simply impossible. What can you do to overcome this dysfunctional pattern in relationships?

Perception filters obscure clear communication

At my retreat I make visual to you what happens when you get engaged in a certain situation where there is a difference of vision or opinion. On a screen I can show you a graphical representation of how you look at the situation. I can show you how your vision is colored. I can illustrate this graphically.

If you want a crude analogy, imagine that I show you a scenery of a beautiful landscape. I then have you put on a pair of colored glasses. You have seen the landscape *without* the glasses and you see it *with* the glasses so you see how your individualized perception has colored what you see. Then I show you another set of glasses, namely the glasses your partner is wearing, and now you see how the same landscape appears to your partner. You see how *your* glasses filter out certain aspects of the scenery so that you simply do not see them. The glasses also emphasize certain other aspects so that they seem much more important to you. We can map this graphically: What is it that your perception filters out and what is it that it emphasizes?

Then I show you a map of the situation with your partner as it is without any coloring. Then we show the map of *your* perception: What is filtered out and what is emphasized. Then I show you a map of *your partner's* perception: What is filtered out and what is emphasized. You can see that in certain situations, what your perception filter emphasizes (so it seems very important) is completely blocked by your partner's perception filter.

How can you ever come to an understanding when your partner cannot even see what you think is very important? You are, as you have so often experienced, talking past each other. It is like you are not even talking the same language. Well, you *are,* in terms of English, French or Latin, but your are not talking a language that helps you come to an understanding. Now you see why this is so, and when you begin to truly internalize what this means, you can begin (in your waking consciousness) to see how to improve communication with your partner.

It starts with overcoming the dysfunctional belief that it should be possible for your partner to see things the way you see them. Then comes going beyond the dysfunctional belief that it would be beneficial if your partner could see things your way. Then you can build a respect for the fact that your partner is not meant to see things your way because your partner will always see things through his or her perception filter—and it will always be *individualized.* Instead of going into a power game of forcing your partner to see things your way, you can avoid using force. What happens in so many talks between partners? One partner gets upset and wants the other partner to see things his or her way. The person then tries to use blame, guilt or some other fear-based emotion to get the other person to accept its own perception.

Does this ever work? Does this ever lead to good communication? Obviously, it does not so why would you want to continue to repeat these patterns? The only way to break out of them is to respect that your partner is not meant to see things your way. Your partner is meant to see things his or her way. What you *can* do is express to your partner how you see things, what you feel about the situation. You can also seek to help your partner clarify how he or she sees or feels about the situation.

Clarifying the communication between partners

Most people are not very clear about what they feel or how they look at a certain situation. You can help your partner gain clarity, but you cannot do this by seeking to force your partner to see things your way. You have to choose whether you want your partner to see things your way or to see things more clearly based on his or her individualized perception.

If you choose the latter, you can build a foundation for constructive communication. If both partners choose this way, you can have a constructive communication that can help you resolve the tension and the conflict because none of you are seeking to force the other to see things "my way." You can come to accept each others differences as a positive, as a catalyst for growth.

It may also be that by clarifying your communication and developing respect for each others communication, you realize that you are simply very different. Then you have a choice to make. Can you build a new relationship based on the acceptance of your differences? Can you overcome this impossible desire to find a partner who is exactly like you and who always sees things your way? Can you accept a partner who is different, see it as a source of growth and then use it constructively? It may be that you come to the honest realization that your partner is so different that either you cannot live together in a constructive relationship, or you are so different that you cannot support each others Divine plans.

It may be legitimate to split up and go your separate ways based on this clarified communication. Then you can do so with a greater degree of peace and harmony than if the relationship splits apart because of dysfunctional communication.

I seek to take students and help them clarify their communication, their perception of truth and their ability to communicate openly. When I have worked with a student for a while, I will make an attempt to help the student begin to see the real issue, the deeper issue, of all human communication. This can be very difficult to grasp for many students.

Before I go into that, let me say this: If it were possible that a husband and wife came to my retreat at the same time and were at the same level of consciousness, I would be able to work with them together so that they would be able (in their waking consciousness) to resolve many things in their relationship. In practical reality, it is very rare that a husband and wife are at the same level of consciousness at the same time.

When you come to the fifth level at my retreat, your spouse is likely at a lower level but can in rare cases be at a higher level than you are. This makes it very difficult for your spouse to accept what *you* can accept about communication, and that makes it necessary for you to have some forbearance and patience with your spouse. Even if you manage to take into your conscious awareness what you learn at my retreat, you cannot demand that your spouse should be able to step up if your spouse is several steps of consciousness below you. Again, there is a need for patience.

The deeper issue of human communication

What is the deeper issue of human communication? What is it that so often blocks communication? You have an outer standard that makes you think that harmony in relationships is based on sameness. At this level, still far below the 144th level, you have elements of the ego and the ego will always feel threatened by differences.

You have a goal with two aspects. The "what" is a harmonious relationship, and then you have the "how," meaning how you can achieve that goal. You think it can be done only through sameness by making your partner like you, finding a partner who is like you or making your partner see things the way you do. You think that if you both see things the same way, you will have a harmonious relationship. In reality, you would have a dead relationship where there would be no growth.

The issue in human relationships is that you attempt to establish a permanent state of some edenic quality in the material world. The deeper reality, that we seek to help you recognize throughout this course, is that the material world is always in a state of transition—*and this is good!*

Embrace the transition! Embrace the changes. Flow with the River of Life. Do not seek to stop anything on earth at a particular state. Do not seek happiness in the outer conditions in the world. Seek happiness within, in flowing with the River of Life.

If you are always trying to communicate based on the idea that you should have harmony, then you will likely attempt to use force to get your partner to see things your way. Or you will fall into the other pattern that is so common in human communication, namely that you do not say something because you do not want to upset your partner.

The real issue in human communications is that you are hardly ever in a situation where you can speak freely with another human being. This is such a prevalent condition on earth that most students do not even have the vision or the belief that it could be possible to communicate freely with another human being. This is based on your experience. You come together with other people, you say something that you think is perfectly innocent, and then, suddenly, the other person takes offence to this and becomes very upset. You sit there, not understanding why the other person reacted this way.

When you have experienced this any number of times from parents, siblings, teachers, spouses and children, then you build a pattern where you do not feel you can express yourself freely. You are always trying to evaluate how the other person will react before you say something. How can you then have free communication?

Strive for free communication

I would give you a different goal. If you are in a relationship, do not make it your goal to create a harmonious relationship. Make it your goal to strive for a state where the two of you can express yourselves freely.

Seek to help each other come to the point where each of you is not reacting to the other through the ego. Seek to make it a goal to give the other person the freedom to express himself or herself freely, without you going into a negative reaction. Give each other the freedom of freedom of speech.

Think about the concept of freedom of speech that is supposedly guaranteed by the constitution of democratic nations. How free is speech in any society when you can say something, and you get a negative reaction that is very unpleasant to you? Do you really have total freedom to say anything you want? I am not saying that it is possible in a society to have complete freedom to say anything you want without getting a reaction from some people.

I am not saying that, in a relationship between two people, you should be able to say anything you want without the other person reacting to it. You *can* make it a goal to give each other the freedom to say anything you want, and then give each other the freedom to say anything you want back based on your own reaction.

If you make an effort, you can get to a point where, even though the other person says something that causes a reaction in you, you are not responding in a fear-based manner. What you can do is to say: "My spouse said something. I feel a reaction in me, but instead of expressing that reaction by being upset, I will step back and I will now describe my reaction to my spouse." It is one thing that you get angry, and then you express that anger in words. It is another if you get angry, and then you step outside the anger, saying to the spouse: "Let me describe to you what I feel based on what you said."

That way, you can take some of the tension out of the communication. The one spouse can say whatever he or she wants and you do not have to suppress your reaction, which would not be a healthy pattern. Instead, you can describe your reaction and you have the freedom to do this. This will make your spouse realize that, when it expresses itself a certain way, it creates a certain reaction in you. You can then begin to look at the reaction and see if there is a way to help you overcome it.

In many cases, you will discover that your spouse had no idea that you reacted this way or why you reacted this way. Your partner had no desire to make you angry (or whatever feeling you have). You can begin to talk about this. You can begin to talk about why your spouse had the need to say what was said that made you angry. What is your spouse's pattern for saying this? How does your spouse react when you are angry, when you express anger? You can gradually build this greater understanding where you are not reacting to each other with a fear-based reaction of feeling threatened or feeling rejected.

The outcome of dysfunctional communication

What is the outcome of this dysfunctional communication where you think you have to get your spouse to see things your way? I have said that it is absolutely impossible to ever make your spouse see things your way so it will never happen. What do you feel when your spouse does not see things your way? You feel rejected!

By building the kind of communication, free communication, that I am talking about, you can get to the point where none of the partners feel rejected when they are not understood. You can even come to the point where you can begin to see that it is actually an asset that your partner does not see things your way. It gives you a wider perspective and helps you expand your sense of self and your ability to react in constructive ways.

When we look at relationships on earth at my retreat, it is so easy to see how often communication is blocked. So many times the two partners sit there, they sense a tension between them and either one or both simply clam up and do not dare to express themselves. This only builds tension. It accumulates fear-based energy because when you suppress your feelings, you generate fear-based energy.

Why are you suppressing your feelings? You are afraid of the reaction you will get when you express them so what suppresses them is fear. You are so afraid of the reaction that your fear is stronger than your feeling so you repress the feeling. This builds up more and more tension. It creates resentment towards your partner because you are seeing things in such a way that it is your partner's fault that you cannot express yourself. Is it really your partners fault, or is it just the dysfunctional dynamics of how relationships have been set up to fail by current conditions on earth? Can you begin to step out of this, become consciously aware of this, and work with each other until you can allow each other the freedom to say what the other person needs to say and then allow you to say what you need to say in response? Instead of reacting in a fear-based downward spiral that only builds more blocks to your communication, you can gradually build an upward spiral that opens up the flow of communication between you.

Harmonious relationships and free communication

My beloved, you may have a dream of a harmonious relationship, but it can never be achieved by suppressing communication. It can never be achieved if both partners, or even one of the partners, cannot speak freely. If you can come to a point where both of you can speak freely, you may actually have a harmonious relationship but one that still leads to growth. If you can set each other free, then each of you will set yourself free and then you will not have the tension. Is it not tension that takes away harmony?

You do not build harmony through sameness. You build it through the free flow of communication that allows the differences to be freely expressed without creating tension. This is what we seek to help you learn at the fifth level of my retreat.

Your spouse is not likely to be at the same level, but your spouse may still be open to some of these ideas. You may be able to use these ideas in your conscious waking awareness to improve communication in all of your relationships. Again, you may encounter a situation where the other person will not change, but that is just an opportunity for you to continue to expand your ability to communicate freely. You will eventually flow on to a different situation.

Do you see what I am attempting to teach here? Do not force things in a relationship. Work on yourself, continue to work on yourself, regardless of how your partner reacts. Then you will tie yourself more and more to the flow of the River of Life until you will one day be able to just let go of your ties to a certain situation and flow on, whatever that means in the physical.

Your Divine plan is much more important to you than any particular relationship. If two people are both on the spiritual path, they should be able to accept this for each other. You cannot expect or demand that your partner should set aside or suppress an important aspect of his or her Divine plan in order to maintain what you see as the right or the harmonious relationship. If both of you have a clear vision of your Divine plan, you might see how both of you can fulfill your Divine plan while you maintain a relationship. Or you might see that you cannot both fulfill your Divine plan while maintaining a relationship, and then you can separate in harmony, understanding and acceptance.

As you expand your vision and realize that your vision is not ultimate truth, you will be more free to flow and to let other people flow. This is the basis for beginning to serve life, rather than thinking life should serve you—or rather: your ego and its dualistic, self-centered perception. This is, of course, the topic for the initiations of the next level, those of the sixth ray.

For now, I bid you contemplate the joy of having completely free communication with another human being. It can be a very fulfilling experience. I AM Paul the Venetian.

13 | I INVOKE TRUTH TO FREE COMMUNICATION

In the name I AM THAT I AM, Jesus Christ, I call to my I AM Presence to flow through the I Will Be Presence that I AM and give this invocation with full power. I call to beloved Elohim Heros and Amora and Cyclopea and Virginia, Archangel Chamuel and Charity and Raphael and Mother Mary, Paul the Venetian and Master Hilarion to help us establish a free form of communication without tension or blockages. Help us see and surrender all patterns that block our oneness with Paul the Venetian and with our I AM Presences, including ...

[Make personal calls]

1. We respect individual perception

1. Paul the Venetian, help us overcome the perversion of love that makes us think there is only one truth and that loving someone means we must get them to see our truth.

O Heros-Amora, in your love so pink,
I care not what others about me may think,
in oneness with you, I claim a new day,
an innocent child, I frolic and play.

O Heros-Amora, a new life begun,
I laugh at the devil, the serious one,
I bathe in your glorious Ruby-Pink Sun,
knowing my God allows life to be fun.

2. Paul the Venetian, help us grasp that none of us can see absolute or unconditional truth through our soul vehicles. We can only see an individualized version of truth.

O Heros-Amora, life is such a joy,
I see that the world is like a great toy,
whatever my mind into it projects,
the mirror of life exactly reflects.

O Heros-Amora, I reap what I sow,
yet this is Plan B for helping me grow,
for truly, Plan A is that I join the flow,
immersed in the Infinite Love you bestow.

3. Paul the Venetian, help us see how the natural desire for truth gets perverted into the desire for an absolute truth and how this sets the stage for relationship problems.

O Heros-Amora, conditions you burn,
I know I AM free to take a new turn,
Immersed in the stream of infinite Love,
I know that my Spirit came from Above.

O Heros-Amora, awakened I see,
in true love is no conditionality,
the devil is stuck in his duality,
but I AM set free by Love's reality.

4. Paul the Venetian, help us acknowledge that what we can see now is a product of our current level of consciousness and the individuality of our soul vehicles.

O Heros-Amora, I feel that at last,
I've risen above the trap of my past,
in true love I claim my freedom to grow,
forever I'm one with Love's Infinite Flow.

O Heros-Amora, conditions are ties,
forming a net of serpentine lies,
your love has no bounds, forever it flies,
raising all life into Ruby-Pink skies.

5. Paul the Venetian, help us escape the trap of thinking that when we love somebody and desire to help them, the only way is to make them see truth as we see it.

Cyclopea so dear, the truth you reveal,
the truth that duality's ailments will heal,
your Emerald Light is like a great balm,
my emotional body is perfectly calm.

Cyclopea so dear, in Emerald Sphere,
to vision so clear I always adhere,
in raising perception I shall persevere,
as deep in my heart your truth I revere.

6. Paul the Venetian, help us respect that another person will not grow by coming to see things the way we see it. The person will grow by gaining a clearer perception based on its own individuality.

Cyclopea so dear, with you I unwind,
all negative spirals clouding my mind,
I know pure awareness is truly my core,
the key to becoming the wide-open door.

Cyclopea so dear, clear my inner sight,
empowered, I pierce the soul's fearful night,
through veils of duality I now take flight,
bathed in your penetrating Emerald Light.

7. Paul the Venetian, help us escape the ego's never-ending desire to make its individualized perception universal by getting all other people to accept it as the truth.

Cyclopea so dear, life can only reflect,
the images that my mind does project,
the key to my healing is clearing the mind,
from the images my ego is hiding behind.

Cyclopea so dear, I want to aim high,
to your healing flame I ever draw nigh,
I now see my life through your single eye,
beyond all disease I AM ready to fly.

8. Paul the Venetian, help us see how our soul vehicles affect our vision. Help us step outside of the perception filter of the soul vehicle and experience a higher reality.

Cyclopea so dear, your Emerald Flame,
exposes every subtle, dualistic power game,
including the game of wanting to say,
that truth is defined in only one way.

Cyclopea so dear, I am feeling the flow,
as your Living Truth upon me you bestow,
I know truth transcends all systems below,
immersed in your light, I continue to grow.

9. Paul the Venetian, help us see and fully accept that our spouse in a love relationship will never come to see life exactly the way we see it.

Accelerate into Oneness, I AM real,
Accelerate into Oneness, all life heal,
Accelerate into Oneness, I AM MORE,
Accelerate into Oneness, all will soar.

Accelerate into Oneness! (3X)
Beloved Heros and Amora.
Accelerate into Oneness! (3X)
Beloved Chamuel and Charity.
Accelerate into Oneness! (3X)
Beloved Paul the Venetian.
Accelerate into Oneness! (3X)
Beloved I AM.

2. We want growth in our relationship

1. Paul the Venetian, help us accept that we are attracted to a certain partner because that person can help us see our own unresolved psychology by making it visible.

Chamuel Archangel, in ruby ray power,
I know I am taking a life-giving shower.
Love burning away all perversions of will,
I suddenly feel my desires falling still.

Chamuel Archangel, descend from Above,
Chamuel Archangel, with ruby-pink love,
Chamuel Archangel, so often thought-of,
Chamuel Archangel, o come Holy Dove.

2. Paul the Venetian, help us accept that our partners make our unresolved psychology visible by getting us to react, not by getting us to see things the way our partners see them.

Chamuel Archangel, a spiral of light,
as ruby ray fire now pierces the night.
All forces of darkness consumed by your fire,
consuming all those who will not rise higher.

Chamuel Archangel, descend from Above,
Chamuel Archangel, with ruby-pink love,
Chamuel Archangel, so often thought-of,
Chamuel Archangel, o come Holy Dove.

3. Paul the Venetian, help us grasp that we need to look at our reaction to our partner in order to discover our own unresolved psychology.

Chamuel Archangel, your love so immense,
with clarified vision, my life now makes sense.
The purpose of life you so clearly reveal,
immersed in your love, God's oneness I feel.

Chamuel Archangel, descend from Above,
Chamuel Archangel, with ruby-pink love,
Chamuel Archangel, so often thought-of,
Chamuel Archangel, o come Holy Dove.

4. Paul the Venetian, help us overcome the trap of thinking that in an ideal relationship, both partners should look at things exactly the same way.

Chamuel Archangel, what calmness you bring,
I see now that even death has no sting.
For truly, in love there can be no decay,
as love is transcendence into a new day.

Chamuel Archangel, descend from Above,
Chamuel Archangel, with ruby-pink love,
Chamuel Archangel, so often thought-of,
Chamuel Archangel, o come Holy Dove.

5. Paul the Venetian, help us avoid seeing our different perspectives as a threat and instead see them as an opportunity to broaden our perspective.

Raphael Archangel, your light so intense,
raise me beyond all human pretense.
Mother Mary and you have a vision so bold,
to see that our highest potential unfold.

Raphael Archangel, for vision I pray,
Raphael Archangel, show me the way,
Raphael Archangel, your emerald ray,
Raphael Archangel, my life a new day.

6. Paul the Venetian, help us grasp that when another person perceives a situation differently, it is an opportunity to expand our sense of self.

Raphael Archangel, in emerald sphere,
to immaculate vision I always adhere.
Mother Mary enfolds me in her sacred heart,
from Mother's true love, I am never apart.

Raphael Archangel, for vision I pray,
Raphael Archangel, show me the way,
Raphael Archangel, your emerald ray,
Raphael Archangel, my life a new day.

7. Paul the Venetian, help us grasp that in order to have a harmonious relationship, we need to recognize that our perception is individualized and that our partner should not accept our perception.

Raphael Archangel, all ailments you heal,
each cell in my body in light now you seal.
Mother Mary's immaculate concept I see,
perfection of health is real now for me.

Raphael Archangel, for vision I pray,
Raphael Archangel, show me the way,
Raphael Archangel, your emerald ray,
Raphael Archangel, my life a new day.

8. Paul the Venetian, help us accept that our partner should expand his or her individualized vision, but it should be allowed to be individualized.

Raphael Archangel, your light is so real,
the vision of Christ in me you reveal.
Mother Mary now helps me to truly transcend,
in emerald light with you I ascend.

Raphael Archangel, for vision I pray,
Raphael Archangel, show me the way,
Raphael Archangel, your emerald ray,
Raphael Archangel, my life a new day.

9. Paul the Venetian, help us allow each other to grow in our own ways so we can have a harmonious relationship that still provides growth.

With angels I soar,
as I reach for MORE.
The angels so real,
their love all will heal.
The angels bring peace,
all conflicts will cease.
With angels of light,
we soar to new height.

The rustling sound of angel wings,
what joy as even matter sings,
what joy as every atom rings,
in harmony with angel wings.

3. We accept our differences

1. Paul the Venetian, help us see how to improve communication by overcoming the tendency to force each other to see things a certain way.

Master Paul, venetian dream,
your love for beauty's flowing stream.
Master Paul, in love's own womb,
your power shatters ego's tomb.

O Holy Spirit, flow through me,
I am the open door for thee.
O mighty rushing stream of Light,
transcendence is my sacred right.

2. Paul the Venetian, help us give each other space to express how we see things, allowing each other to clarify how we feel about the situation.

Master Paul, your counsel wise,
my mind is raised to lofty skies.
Master Paul, in wisdom's love,
such beauty flowing from Above.

O Holy Spirit, flow through me,
I am the open door for thee.
O mighty rushing stream of Light,
transcendence is my sacred right.

3. Paul the Venetian, help us build a foundation for constructive communication that can help us resolve the tension and conflict between us.

Master Paul, love is an art,
it opens up the secret heart.
Master Paul, love's rushing flow,
my heart awash in sacred glow.

O Holy Spirit, flow through me,
I am the open door for thee.
O mighty rushing stream of Light,
transcendence is my sacred right.

4. Paul the Venetian, help us accept each others differences as a positive, as a catalyst for growth.

Master Paul, accelerate,
upon pure love I meditate.
Master Paul, intentions pure,
my self-transcendence will ensure.

O Holy Spirit, flow through me,
I am the open door for thee.
O mighty rushing stream of Light,
transcendence is my sacred right.

5. Paul the Venetian, help us build a new relationship based on the acceptance of our differences. Help us each overcome the impossible desire to find a partner who is exactly like us and who always sees things our way.

Master Paul, your love will heal,
my inner light you do reveal.
Master Paul, all life console,
with you I'm being truly whole.

O Holy Spirit, flow through me,
I am the open door for thee.
O mighty rushing stream of Light,
transcendence is my sacred right.

6. Paul the Venetian, help us accept a partner who is different, see it as a source of growth and use it constructively.

Master Paul, you serve the All,
by helping us transcend the fall.
Master Paul, in peace we rise,
as ego meets its sure demise.

O Holy Spirit, flow through me,
I am the open door for thee.
O mighty rushing stream of Light,
transcendence is my sacred right.

7. Paul the Venetian, help us overcome the illusion that harmony in relationships is based on sameness. Help us see that only the ego is threatened by differences.

Master Paul, love all life free,
your love is for eternity.
Master Paul, you are the One,
to help us make the journey fun.

O Holy Spirit, flow through me,
I am the open door for thee.
O mighty rushing stream of Light,
transcendence is my sacred right.

8. Paul the Venetian, help us overcome the pattern of using force to get our partner to agree.

Master Paul, you balance all,
the seven rays upon my call.
Master Paul, you paint the sky,
with colors that delight the I.

O Holy Spirit, flow through me,
I am the open door for thee.
O mighty rushing stream of Light,
transcendence is my sacred right.

9. Paul the Venetian, help us overcome the pattern where we don't say something because we don't want to upset our partner.

Master Paul, your Presence here,
filling up my inner sphere.
Life is now a sacred flow,
God Love I do on all bestow.

O Holy Spirit, flow through me,
I am the open door for thee.
O mighty rushing stream of Light,
transcendence is my sacred right.

4. We give each other freedom of speech

1. Paul the Venetian, help us see how to achieve a state where both of us can express ourselves freely. Help us avoid reacting to each other through the ego.

Hilarion, on emerald shore,
I'm free from all that's gone before.
Hilarion, I let all go,
that keeps me out of sacred flow.

O Holy Spirit, flow through me,
I am the open door for thee.
O mighty rushing stream of Light,
transcendence is my sacred right.

2. Paul the Venetian, help us give each other the space to express ourselves freely without having to fear a negative reaction from the other person.

Hilarion, the secret key,
is wisdom's own reality.
Hilarion, all life is healed,
the ego's face no more concealed.

O Holy Spirit, flow through me,
I am the open door for thee.
O mighty rushing stream of Light,
transcendence is my sacred right.

3. Paul the Venetian, help us give each other the freedom where one person can say anything he or she wants, and the other person is free to say anything back based on his or her reaction.

Hilarion, your love for life,
helps me surrender inner strife.
Hilarion, your loving words,
thrill my heart like song of birds.

O Holy Spirit, flow through me,
I am the open door for thee.
O mighty rushing stream of Light,
transcendence is my sacred right.

4. Paul the Venetian, help us learn how to never speak based on a fear-based reaction but to describe the reaction to the other person.

Hilarion, invoke the light,
your sacred formulas recite.
Hilarion, your secret tone,
philosopher's most sacred stone.

O Holy Spirit, flow through me,
I am the open door for thee.
O mighty rushing stream of Light,
transcendence is my sacred right.

5. Paul the Venetian, help us build a greater understanding where we are not reacting to each other with a fear-based reaction of feeling threatened or feeling rejected.

Hilarion, with love you greet,
me in your temple over Crete.
Hilarion, your emerald light,
my third eye sees with Christic sight.

O Holy Spirit, flow through me,
I am the open door for thee.
O mighty rushing stream of Light,
transcendence is my sacred right.

6. Paul the Venetian, help us develop a relationship where none of us feel rejected when we are not understood.

Hilarion, you give me fruit,
of truth that is so absolute.
Hilarion, all stress decrease,
as my ambitions I release.

O Holy Spirit, flow through me,
I am the open door for thee.
O mighty rushing stream of Light,
transcendence is my sacred right.

7. Paul the Venetian, help us allow each other the freedom to say what we need to say, thereby building an upward spiral that opens up the flow of communication between us.

Hilarion, my chakras clear,
as I let go of subtlest fear.
Hilarion, I am sincere,
as freedom's truth I do revere.

O Holy Spirit, flow through me,
I am the open door for thee.
O mighty rushing stream of Light,
transcendence is my sacred right.

8. Paul the Venetian, help us see that having a harmonious relationship can never be achieved by suppressing communication, but only when both of us can speak freely.

Hilarion, you balance all,
the seven rays upon my call.
Hilarion, you keep me true,
as I remain all one with you.

O Holy Spirit, flow through me,
I am the open door for thee.
O mighty rushing stream of Light,
transcendence is my sacred right.

9. Paul the Venetian, help us grasp that we do not build harmony through sameness, we build it through the free flow of communication that allows differences to be expressed freely without creating tension.

Hilarion, your Presence here,
filling up my inner sphere.
Life is now a sacred flow,
God Vision I on all bestow.

O Holy Spirit, flow through me,
I am the open door for thee.
O mighty rushing stream of Light,
transcendence is my sacred right.

Sealing:

In the name of the Divine Mother, I fully accept that the power of these calls is used to set free the Ma-ter light, so it can outpicture the perfect vision of Christ for my own life, for all people and for the planet. In the name I AM THAT I AM, it is done! Amen.

14 | LOVE AND SERVICE

I AM Paul the Venetian, the Chohan of the Third Ray of Divine Love. When you come to the sixth level of my retreat, you face the initiation of love combined with the Sixth Ray of Peace and Service. Before you can serve to the maximum capacity, you must have attained peace so let us deal with the perversions of love as they relate to peace.

The worldly view of love

When most people come to my retreat, as they are engaged in the path of self-mastery, they have been deeply affected by the worldly view of love. You have on planet earth so many manifestations of anti-love, especially the manifestations of anti-peace and aggression of the power players who are exercising power and abusing power. Having grown up for lifetimes experiencing this, being on the receiving end of the power people, you naturally look for an alternative. Deep within, you have the sense that love is part of that alternative. You even have certain philosophies floating around that say: "Love conquers all. Love is the great healer. Love is all you need," and all of this stuff.

So many people have come to believe in the philosophy, that is floating around in the collective consciousness of the planet, which says that love is the opposite of power because love is always gentle and kind and pink and soft. You think that love is peaceful, in the sense that peace is passive.

We have spoken about the fact that peace is not passive, certainly not pacifying, and neither is love. You cannot attain peace about love until you are willing to express love in all of its facets. Love *can* be gentle and kind, but love is only gentle and kind when that is what people need in order to heal from a trauma, from a wound. There is a lot of use, on a planet as warring as earth, for that kind of gentle love. This is not in dispute. I am not saying it is wrong to express this kind of love.

What I *am* saying is that you cannot find peace in your expression of love unless you realize that love, the core of love, is to help people transcend and become more. If people need a more direct, a more stern, a more intense, action of love, then that is what we of the ascended masters will release. If you are to be at peace in serving on the path of self-mastery, serving others, you must be able to be an open door also for the more direct expressions of love.

Learning the facets of love

All of the rays have a certain range, which you can see even in a range of visible colors. Most people think of love as only pink, but the range goes all the way to the most intense, laser-like, ruby fire. So many students come to my retreat at this level and think that love must be pink. So many people have been brought up with parents or other authority figures abusing their power, which most people have seen as being not loving.

Of course, the abuse of power is not loving. The expression of power in order to awaken you and have you come up higher or realize that you need to stop self-destructive patterns is not an abuse of power. It is loving to help you, as a child, snap out of these self-destructive patterns.

You need to learn to discern between a correct expression of power and an abuse of power. You can learn this by learning the different facets of love. If you only see love as pink, you can never come to acknowledge a correct expression of power. You will see any expression of power that is direct as an abuse of power, and it is not. When you open yourself up to the more ruby ray aspects of love, then you begin to see that intensity can be needed in order to help someone climb over the edge of the downward spiral that the person has been in.

Expressing the intensity of love

What happens when people are in a downward spiral? You can go in, invoke energy, consume the energy that drives the spiral, and thereby slow down the spiral so that they can begin to extricate themselves from it. You can also recognize that when people are in a downward spiral, they are moving. If you can accelerate the movement, you might be able to slingshot them out of the spiral.

Some of you may have experienced in your life that either a parent, a spouse or a guru said one remark that was said with such intensity that it cut through your normal defenses. This caused such a shock to your mind that you were opened to a higher reality. Just that one remark was enough to get you out of a self-destructive pattern and set you on a new course. This is love. This is an expression of love. It may be colored with power, but it is essentially love as opposed to fear.

An abuse of power always springs from fear. A correct use of power is above that level of vibration. It vibrates with love, intense love. Intensity should not be confused with harshness. It is not, but it is immovability. You should know by now that the ego will always seek to move everything towards the lowest common denominator and pacify you. There is sometimes an intensity needed in order to get you out of this pacifying spiral, this pacifying state of consciousness. I have spoken about freedom of communication in relationships, but this can hardly be attained unless the people pass the initiations of the Sixth Ray and realize that love is not always peaceful.

You have a right to be intense with your partner. If you are not coming from fear, if your intensity is based on love, then this is – or ideally should be – allowed in a relationship. It should be seen as an asset to the relationship if one or even both of the partners can reach a certain intensity. It is, of course, important that you are willing to look at yourself and see if you have patterns that are not love-based intensity but fear-based abuse of power. Yelling at your partner in anger or fear is not constructive to building a relationship.

Free communication is not abuse of power

It may be necessary for some time period that you can express yourself freely and that your partner can learn to endure this. You can then work through whatever pattern you have, making it visible to yourself and to your partner, so that you may discuss it freely. What I am talking about here is not the dysfunctional patterns seen in so many relationships, namely that one partner gets upset and starts yelling, and the other shuts down and withdraws into a shell.

If you have established freedom of communication, then you can allow one partner to express whatever feelings are there in the subconscious. The purpose of doing this is to make them visible and thereby start transforming them, discovering the pattern and the illusion behind them so that you can transcend it. It is not the intent behind having free communication that the one person can continue to express fear-based emotions indefinitely without ever working on them.

My beloved, love is not all you need—if you see love as the soft, pink, passive love. If you can master all facets of love, then you can say that love is all you need because then love incorporates all of the seven rays in all of their aspects. All you need in the material universe is all of the seven rays. You can ascend by mastering the seven rays. It certainly helps to master the Eighth Ray of Integration and even some of the secret rays, but you can qualify for your ascension by attaining mastery on the seven rays. The seven rays is all you need.

Many relationships are locked in a pattern where both of the partners feel they always have to be gentle. This is especially true for spiritual people where both partners in a relationship have discovered the spiritual path and perhaps have walked it for some time. It is especially the case for people who have delved into certain Eastern teachings.

The Eastern teachings very much encourage you to go within. Whether it be yoga or different forms of meditation, contemplation or mindfulness, it is all about finding stillness within. I am not saying this is wrong, but if you chose to be born in the West, you might contemplate that the Eastern model of you sitting in a cave and holding a spiritual balance through the peace of your mind is not applicable to the West.

What needs to happen for a golden age to be manifest is that spiritual people all over the world, including in the East, become more active in society. You need to demand, and demonstrate by example, a higher way than the old patterns of non-peace.

Sometimes, someone must be able to express in the spoken word that intensity of the ruby fire. Sometimes, in public debate, it is necessary that someone can stand up and grab people's attention and cut through the miasma that prevents a breakthrough in a certain area. Who will do this if not the spiritual people? Who will do this if you are locked in always seeking to go within, always seeking to be peaceful? How will you establish a truly peaceful relationship unless you overcome all elements of non-peace, of anti-peace?

The perversions of peace

What have I said in my previous discourses? Any God quality has been perverted by the fallen beings by establishing a relative, dualistic polarity. The same with peace. At one end, you have aggression and war. At the other end, you have, supposedly, the person who is completely peaceful and thereby being passive. This is not the Middle Way. This is not the golden, middle way for the golden age. So many spiritual people have locked themselves into thinking this is how they have to always behave, including in their relationships.

You see couples who are very spiritual and participate in many spiritual activities. They have come to a point that is similar to what many couples in the world have reached. They have acknowledged who they are, what wounds and problems they have, and then they avoid stirring up any difficult issues. They have made harmony, peacefulness, such a goal of their relationships that it holds back their growth rather than promoting the growth.

This is not true peace because true peace does not create a static state of peace on this planet. It creates a dynamic peace where there is maximum growth because there is not the concept or the conflict that pulls you into opposing patterns. Such patterns steal your energy and put you on a seesaw between highs and lows that shatter your inner peace, your focus on the I AM Presence.

If both of you are spiritual in a relationship, then be willing to confront the issues, even if it creates a state of disharmony for a time. If you use the tools that we have given, you will be able to work through it. Then you can have a more genuine, and certainly a more growth-oriented, relationship. This might open you up to be able to fulfill your Divine plan in a higher measure because you can now feel free to express the more intense aspects of love. This intensity is the key to true service.

The need for spiritual people in society

The Sixth Ray is peace and service, but the fallen beings have perverted the concept of peace by saying that only those who are peaceful in a pacifying sense are truly serving.

Many people, even many spiritual people, think that in order to give service to life, they have to find some kind of service-oriented work. This may be as doctors, nurses, teachers, aid-workers or many other things. I am in no way condemning people for doing this. There is a great need that spiritual people enter these fields.

I am only pointing out that if you think these are the only kind of fields that spiritual people can be in, then you may be closing the door with the conscious mind to the fulfillment of your Divine plan. You are applying an overlay to yourself that might close your mind to an awareness of what is in your Divine plan.

There is a need for spiritual people in all areas of society. Certainly, there are some occupations you might avoid, such as anything that has to do with crime, anything illegal or any kind of manipulation.

Even in the business world – as perverted as it can be in many cases – there is a need for people who are spiritual but know the business world from the inside. They can therefore be an instrument for expressing new ideas, even the intensity that sometimes is needed in order to cut through both in specific situations (in a particular business) or in terms of helping society develop a new approach to business or to money.

There is a need for a new money system, which we have talked about. It will not come about only through passive measures. Someone must carry that Ruby Fire to cut through the opposition, the incredibly intense opposition, in order to manifest a money system that actually benefits the people rather than the elite.

Overcoming your reactions to accusations

When you come to the sixth level of my retreat, you need to face a very difficult test. You need to face the test of learning not to be affected by the accusations of the fallen consciousness. How can you be at peace on a planet like earth if the fallen beings can come in and accuse you of something and then you have immediately lost your peace? The specific initiation you face at my retreat is to learn how to deal with a situation where you are accused of being not loving because you have dared to express yourself more freely.

We will teach you how to do this. We will show you how you engage in a reactionary pattern when you are accused. We will help you see where that reaction comes from, where the energy spiral is that feeds it. We will help you go into that spiral, go to the bottom of it and see the illusion. Then you can look at the spirit and say: "Get thee behind me, Satan. You have nothing in me anymore."

So many well-meaning people have entered some form of public service. They have taken a stand for some kind of change, some kind of new idea. They have met the inevitable opposition from people who are trapped in the fallen consciousness. There is no area on earth where you can suggest a new idea or a positive change without running into people who are so trapped in the fallen consciousness that they will resist any change.

So many people have encountered this resistance, have reacted in a defensive manner or have reacted by becoming more intense, possibly abusing power. As soon as they have done this, those in the fallen consciousness have accused these people of not being peaceful, not being loving, not being kind, not being true servants, only trying to create trouble—or others of the many accusations that people trapped in the fallen consciousness can come up with. There is no point in listing them because there are so many they would fill several books.

So many well-meaning people, who had the potential in their Divine plans to help bring about change, have been so shocked, distraught and disturbed by this reaction that they have withdrawn from public service.

You see it all the time. The good people cannot stand being in the dysfunctional, accusatory environment that exists in so many areas on earth. Why do you think all of the people in politics are the way they are? There is a filter of unnatural selection that filters out all of the kind and loving people but also those who are loving in an intense way. Nobody who is a positive person can stand being in politics in many nations. You have only those left who are so trapped in the fallen consciousness and so driven by ambition that they will endure anything in order to gain power.

What is the key to avoiding this reaction. It is to tune in to the core of love, which is the drive to help people transcend and become more. This drive is balanced with respect for free will. What often makes you frustrated when you engage in some kind of public service is that you have a clear vision of how things should be improved. You are working towards a specific physical change. When you meet people who resist this, who refuse to see things your way, you go into a defensive reaction. At some point, you have had enough of their opposition and their accusations, and you say: "Then I will just leave you alone and you can do whatever you want."

Presenting people with the opportunity to choose

This is exactly what those in the fallen consciousness want. They have done this so many times before, and they know exactly how to push people's buttons and drive them into this reaction. In order to avoid this pattern, you need to recognize that love does not want to produce certain physical results on this planet. Love only wants to present people with a choice to self-transcend. When you go into an area of public service and you present some kind of new idea or change, you have given the other people who are involved an opportunity to choose the higher or the lower.

With your conscious mind you may think that if they do not choose the higher, then your service has failed. I am a Chohan and I do not look at it that way. I do not see that your effort has failed, for what have you done? You have given people a choice they did not have before. You have forced them to choose, which is your right within free will because you are in physical embodiment. Whether they choose the high road or the low road, you have still given a service.

It is true that, if they choose the low road, the outer results you were working for will not be manifest. There *will* be a result because they will move one step closer to their judgment and to the point where they will be removed from this earth [For more about these topics, see *Cosmology of Evil*]. In the long run, your effort will have a positive impact on the planet. You have given a valuable service and you should be content with presenting people with a choice and leaving it up to them what they will do with it. That way, you can avoid tying your continued service to the achievement of particular results.

Think back to what I already said about truth, about not getting your partner to see things your way but allowing your partner to see it his or her way. The same goes in public service. There are people who may be in the fallen consciousness, or they may be in a lower state of consciousness where they cannot grasp your higher vision. *They* have a right to be where they are at in consciousness. *You* have a right to be where you are at. You have a right to express your vision, but they also have a right to respond to your expression based on their state of consciousness.

Certainly, they have a right to use your higher vision to transcend their state of consciousness, but if they are not willing to do this, they have a right to refuse. You do not have a right to react negatively when other people exercise their free will. You should – this is *your* responsibility – have gotten yourself into a state of mind where you are not demanding that other people make a certain choice. You are content with presenting them with the opportunity to choose.

This is how you give higher service: Not by producing a certain physical result, but by presenting people with an opportunity to choose something that is higher than their present level of consciousness. This is all that we of the Chohans are doing.

If you think that we, the seven Chohans and the Maha Chohan, are sitting up here with elaborate plans for how every little detail should be changed at the physical level, then you do not understand us. Certainly, Saint Germain has a plan for the golden age. It is not set in stone. It is not worked out in minute details. The golden age is not something that can be forced upon humankind. It must be chosen.

Saint Germain has a plan for how he can present humankind with higher ideas that give them the opportunity to choose. Saint Germain does not demand a specific result manifest at a specific date. Saint Germain has reached Buddhic attainment. He knows that if the golden age is not manifest in a certain way today, then it might be tomorrow or in a century.

Balancing decisive action and patience

It may be urgent that you make a certain change in your life at a certain time. It may be urgent for you to make an effort to come up higher in consciousness within a very short period of time because there is a certain element of your Divine plan that you need to be ready to start fulfilling at a certain time. You may even have to be very intense in order to qualify for your ascension in this lifetime. Do not fall prey to the epic mindset that certain outer changes absolutely must happen at a certain time. This will only take you away from peace. It will take you away from love-based service and into fear-based service where you become more and more frustrated until you burn yourself out and can no longer stand it.

There are so many times where we can see that a certain person had in his or her Divine plan to work for a particular change in a particular area of society. Precisely because the person got trapped in the pattern I have described here, of reacting to the fallen consciousness, the person withdrew from that area. If the person, on the other hand, had been able to take the longer view and be more patient, then the person could have achieved significant results over a longer period of time. It may be that the person had never achieved the exact result that was envisioned when the person withdrew, but some significant result would have been attained.

Overcoming the now-or-never consciousness

The world does not progress in huge leaps and bounds. The world progresses in small steps. Each of you are here to make a contribution to these small steps being taken. Once in a while, a person brings forth an idea that has greater ramifications, but most of you are here to bring the world forward in small increments. This means you need to be patient. You need to be peaceful. You need to avoid going into the frustrated mindset where you think that: "This *has* to happen right now. It is now or never!"

It is the ego, the fallen beings and the internal spirits that want you to feel this way. Have you ever gone into a car dealership and been exposed to a trained salesman who is attempting to sell you a used car? They have been trained to create a sense of urgency. If you do not sign the contract right now, you will lose this wonderful offer that they claim they are giving you. Why do you think people go to war? It is because they have been manipulated into a sense of urgency where something has to happen right now! My beloved, it is *never* now or never!

There is a saying in the East: "Men may come, and men may go, but I go on forever." The River of Life goes on forever. Situations may come; situations may go but the River of Life continues to flow. A new opportunity will come. Certainly, there are situations where not taking an opportunity can have severe consequences. This does not mean that the opportunity to learn is lost, and that is what we of the Chohans are looking for.

What have I said is the definition of Satan? Is is that Spirit conforms to current conditions in matter. How will you transcend current conditions? Not by getting yourself into a state where you have been so affected by these conditions that you think they have to be changed right now. They have to be changed in the only way you can see right now that they can be changed. This means that these other people have to do things your way. If they will not do so voluntarily, they must be forced to do so. That is how you start wars and conflicts. That is how communication breaks down.

You have a certain vision right now. It is not the highest possible vision. If you are growing on the path, you will not have that vision for the rest of your life. It may be that right now you have a correct vision of *what* needs to change, but it may also be that you do not have the highest vision of *how* it can be changed. If you present people with the opportunity, as you can see it right now, and they do not choose it, then you don't get frustrated. You go within. You look at your reactions. You avoid a negative pattern. You ask for guidance and direction for how you can come to see this from a higher perspective. Then you just wait for the next opportunity where you might present something from a higher, more mature vision.

At the same time, you know that the planet moves on, and it is in an upward spiral. Even the people who are resisting today may be forced to move on. When the new opportunity comes, they might be more open. Suddenly, the stars are aligned in a different way and there may be an opening that was not there before. If you had gone into the force-based, fear-based reaction previously, then you might have withdrawn from the field. Or you might have built up such animosity from others that they would have been closed to you by now, and the second opportunity would be passed by also.

Conflict is now or never. Peace goes on forever.

Conflict usually arises from the sense of now or never. How can you be an emissary of peace if you have that state of mind? Conflict is now or never; peace goes on forever. Opportunities will come, opportunities will go, but even an opportunity lost is not gone forever. The wheels will turn and a new opportunity will present itself. This is how you learn to serve peacefully.

Love always wants to transcend, but you do not transcend by having the vision that there is an ultimate result that must be manifest. Then you shut off the flow of love. If you can stay outside of that now-or-never mentality, this all-or-nothing, this my-way-or-the-highway mentality, then you can be in the flow of love. You just wait for the next opportunity.

If you never get another opportunity because the other people keep resisting, then you do as I have said before. You focus on your own reaction, and then you may come to the point where you know that now it is not a matter of withdrawing from this field in a huff. It is a matter of naturally flowing into your next level of service, whatever that may be. You may have no vision of this now, and you certainly will never get a vision of it as long as you are in this all-or-nothing state of mind.

How can two people serve each other in a relationship if each has a vision of how the other person should change or how the relationship should be, and they are both in the all-or-nothing, now-or-never mentality? Serving another person is giving the other person an opportunity to grow, not producing a certain outer result. Be patient with yourself and with your partner.

Many of you get so frantic, or you get so tired of conflict, that you say: "I must have peace now!" The way to peace is through patience. Nobody has ever attained peace without going through the doorway of patience, which sometimes requires long-suffering. The length of your suffering depends on how long it takes you to let go of your attachment to outer results. You cannot attain peace as long as you are attached to outer results. It has never been done, my beloved.

You may produce an outer result, but you will not produce it through the attachment to that result, for you are not the doer. The flow of the Spirit, the River of Life, is the doer. You provide the chalice that the flow of love can flow into, and then you let love do its work. Then you are at peace, no matter what the physical outcome. You are at peace in letting love flow and thereby presenting people with an opportunity to choose the higher way, the way of love, the way of peace.

I AM Paul the Venetian.

LOVE

15 | I INVOKE LOVE-BASED SERVICE

In the name I AM THAT I AM, Jesus Christ, I call to my I AM Presence to flow through the I Will Be Presence that I AM and give this invocation with full power. I call to beloved Elohim Heros and Amora and Peace and Aloha, Archangel Chamuel and Charity and Uriel and Aurora, Paul the Venetian and Master Nada to help us give service to life from a state of inner peace. Help us see and surrender all patterns that block our oneness with Paul the Venetian and with our I AM Presences, including …

[Make personal calls]

1. We rise above passive love

1. Paul the Venetian, help us overcome the illusion that love is peaceful in the sense that peace is passive. Help us attain peace about love by being willing to express love in all of its facets.

O Heros-Amora, in your love so pink,
I care not what others about me may think,
in oneness with you, I claim a new day,
an innocent child, I frolic and play.

**O Heros-Amora, a new life begun,
I laugh at the devil, the serious one,
I bathe in your glorious Ruby-Pink Sun,
knowing my God allows life to be fun.**

2. Paul the Venetian, help us realize that the core of love is to help people transcend and become more.

O Heros-Amora, life is such a joy,
I see that the world is like a great toy,
whatever my mind into it projects,
the mirror of life exactly reflects.

**O Heros-Amora, I reap what I sow,
yet this is Plan B for helping me grow,
for truly, Plan A is that I join the flow,
immersed in the Infinite Love you bestow.**

3. Paul the Venetian, help us be the open doors for the more direct expressions of love when we or other people need them.

O Heros-Amora, conditions you burn,
I know I AM free to take a new turn,
Immersed in the stream of infinite Love,
I know that my Spirit came from Above.

O Heros-Amora, awakened I see,
in true love is no conditionality,
the devil is stuck in his duality,
but I AM set free by Love's reality.

4. Paul the Venetian, help us be open to the expression of love-based power in order to awaken each other from self-destructive patterns.

O Heros-Amora, I feel that at last,
I've risen above the trap of my past,
in true love I claim my freedom to grow,
forever I'm one with Love's Infinite Flow.

O Heros-Amora, conditions are ties,
forming a net of serpentine lies,
your love has no bounds, forever it flies,
raising all life into Ruby-Pink skies.

5. Paul the Venetian, help us discern between a correct expression of power and an abuse of power. Help us learn the different facets of love, from pink to ruby.

O Elohim Peace, in Unity's Flame,
there is no more room for duality's game,
we know that all form is from the same source,
empowering us to plot a new course.

O Elohim Peace, the bell now you ring,
causing all atoms to vibrate and sing,
I now see that there is no separate thing,
to my ego-based self I no longer cling.

6. Paul the Venetian, help us attain freedom of communication by passing the initiations of the Sixth Ray and accepting that love is not always peaceful.

O Elohim Peace, you help me to know,
that Jesus has come your Flame to bestow,
upon all who are ready to give up the strife,
by following Christ into infinite life.

O Elohim Peace, through your eyes I see,
that only in oneness will I ever be free,
I give up the sense of a separate me,
I AM crossing Samsara's turbulent sea.

7. Paul the Venetian, help us accept that one has a right to be intense with one's partner. Help us see intensity as an asset to our relationship, and overcome patterns that are not love-based intensity but fear-based abuse of power.

O Elohim Peace, you show me the way,
for clearing my mind from duality's fray,
you pierce the illusions of both time and space,
separation consumed by your Infinite Grace.

O Elohim Peace, what beauty your name,
consuming within me duality's shame,
It was through the vibration of your Golden Flame,
that Christ the illusion of death overcame.

8. Paul the Venetian, help us give each other the freedom to express ourselves freely so we can help each other work through our unresolved psychology without creating a reactionary spiral.

O Elohim Peace, you bring now to earth,
the unstoppable flame of Cosmic Rebirth,
I give up the sense that something is mine,
allowing your Light through my being to shine.

O Elohim Peace, through your tranquility,
we are free from the chaos of duality,
in oneness with God a new identity,
we are raising the earth into Infinity.

9. Paul the Venetian, help us overcome the pattern where one partner gets upset and the other shuts down and withdraws into a shell.

Accelerate into Oneness, I AM real,
Accelerate into Oneness, all life heal,
Accelerate into Oneness, I AM MORE,
Accelerate into Oneness, all will soar.

Accelerate into Oneness! (3X)
Beloved Heros and Amora.
Accelerate into Oneness! (3X)
Beloved Chamuel and Charity.
Accelerate into Oneness! (3X)
Beloved Paul the Venetian.
Accelerate into Oneness! (3X)
Beloved I AM.

2. We express ourselves freely

1. Paul the Venetian, help us allow one of us to express whatever feelings are there in the subconscious for the purpose of making them visible.

Chamuel Archangel, in ruby ray power,
I know I am taking a life-giving shower.
Love burning away all perversions of will,
I suddenly feel my desires falling still.

Chamuel Archangel, descend from Above,
Chamuel Archangel, with ruby-pink love,
Chamuel Archangel, so often thought-of,
Chamuel Archangel, o come Holy Dove.

2. Paul the Venetian, help us transform our subconscious feelings, discovering the pattern and the illusion behind them so we can transcend it.

Chamuel Archangel, a spiral of light,
as ruby ray fire now pierces the night.
All forces of darkness consumed by your fire,
consuming all those who will not rise higher.

Chamuel Archangel, descend from Above,
Chamuel Archangel, with ruby-pink love,
Chamuel Archangel, so often thought-of,
Chamuel Archangel, o come Holy Dove.

3. Paul the Venetian, help us overcome the pattern of feeling we always have to be gentle.

Chamuel Archangel, your love so immense,
with clarified vision, my life now makes sense.
The purpose of life you so clearly reveal,
immersed in your love, God's oneness I feel.

Chamuel Archangel, descend from Above,
Chamuel Archangel, with ruby-pink love,
Chamuel Archangel, so often thought-of,
Chamuel Archangel, o come Holy Dove.

4. Paul the Venetian, help us establish a truly peaceful relationship by overcoming all elements of non-peace, of anti-peace.

Chamuel Archangel, what calmness you bring,
I see now that even death has no sting.
For truly, in love there can be no decay,
as love is transcendence into a new day.

Chamuel Archangel, descend from Above,
Chamuel Archangel, with ruby-pink love,
Chamuel Archangel, so often thought-of,
Chamuel Archangel, o come Holy Dove.

5. Paul the Venetian, help us overcome the desire to always be peaceful so we can dare to acknowledge who we are, what wounds and problems we have.

Uriel Archangel, immense is the power,
of angels of peace, all war to devour.
The demons of war, no match for your light,
consuming them all, with radiance so bright.

Uriel Archangel, use your great sword,
Uriel Archangel, consume all discord,
Uriel Archangel, we're of one accord,
Uriel Archangel, we walk with the Lord.

6. Paul the Venetian, help us be willing to deal with the difficult issues so we can develop a more genuine and growth-oriented relationship that helps us fulfill our Divine plans.

Uriel Archangel, intense is the sound,
when millions of angels, their voices compound.
They build a crescendo, piercing the night,
life's glorious oneness revealed to our sight.

Uriel Archangel, use your great sword,
Uriel Archangel, consume all discord,
Uriel Archangel, we're of one accord,
Uriel Archangel, we walk with the Lord.

7. Paul the Venetian, help us set each other free to express the more intense aspects of love. Help us see that intensity is the key to true service.

Uriel Archangel, from out the Great Throne,
your millions of trumpets, sound the One Tone.
Consuming all discord with your harmony,
the sound of all sounds will set all life free.

Uriel Archangel, use your great sword,
Uriel Archangel, consume all discord,
Uriel Archangel, we're of one accord,
Uriel Archangel, we walk with the Lord.

8. Paul the Venetian, help us learn not to be affected by the accusations of the fallen consciousness. Help us stop accusing each other through this consciousness.

Uriel Archangel, all war is now gone,
for you bring a message, from heart of the One.
The hearts of all men, now singing in peace,
the spirals of love, forever increase.

Uriel Archangel, use your great sword,
Uriel Archangel, consume all discord,
Uriel Archangel, we're of one accord,
Uriel Archangel, we walk with the Lord.

9. Paul the Venetian, help us learn to deal with a situation where we are accused of being not loving because we have dared to express ourselves more freely.

With angels I soar,
as I reach for MORE.
The angels so real,
their love all will heal.
The angels bring peace,
all conflicts will cease.
With angels of light,
we soar to new height.

The rustling sound of angel wings,
what joy as even matter sings,
what joy as every atom rings,
in harmony with angel wings.

3. We are serving each other

1. Paul the Venetian, help us learn how to serve each other by helping each other give the service that is part of our Divine plans.

> Master Paul, venetian dream,
> your love for beauty's flowing stream.
> Master Paul, in love's own womb,
> your power shatters ego's tomb.
>
> **O Holy Spirit, flow through me,**
> **I am the open door for thee.**
> **O mighty rushing stream of Light,**
> **transcendence is my sacred right.**

2. Paul the Venetian, help us see how we engage in a reactionary pattern when we are accused by the fallen consciousness. Help us see the internal spirit behind that reaction.

> Master Paul, your counsel wise,
> my mind is raised to lofty skies.
> Master Paul, in wisdom's love,
> such beauty flowing from Above.
>
> **O Holy Spirit, flow through me,**
> **I am the open door for thee.**
> **O mighty rushing stream of Light,**
> **transcendence is my sacred right.**

3. Paul the Venetian, help us serve each other so we can bring forth new ideas in our field without being destroyed by the opposition from people who are trapped in the fallen consciousness.

Master Paul, love is an art,
it opens up the secret heart.
Master Paul, love's rushing flow,
my heart awash in sacred glow.

O Holy Spirit, flow through me,
I am the open door for thee.
O mighty rushing stream of Light,
transcendence is my sacred right.

4. Paul the Venetian, help us develop total respect for free will, the free will of each other as well as other people.

Master Paul, accelerate,
upon pure love I meditate.
Master Paul, intentions pure,
my self-transcendence will ensure.

O Holy Spirit, flow through me,
I am the open door for thee.
O mighty rushing stream of Light,
transcendence is my sacred right.

5. Paul the Venetian, help us recognize that love does not want to produce certain physical results on this planet. Love only wants to present people with a choice to self-transcend.

Master Paul, your love will heal,
my inner light you do reveal.
Master Paul, all life console,
with you I'm being truly whole.

**O Holy Spirit, flow through me,
I am the open door for thee.
O mighty rushing stream of Light,
transcendence is my sacred right.**

6. Paul the Venetian, help us see that our service is to present people with a real choice. The success of our service does not depend on what other people choose.

Master Paul, you serve the All,
by helping us transcend the fall.
Master Paul, in peace we rise,
as ego meets its sure demise.

**O Holy Spirit, flow through me,
I am the open door for thee.
O mighty rushing stream of Light,
transcendence is my sacred right.**

7. Paul the Venetian, help us accept that we have a right to force other people to choose, but that we must be non-attached to *what* they choose.

Master Paul, love all life free,
your love is for eternity.
Master Paul, you are the One,
to help us make the journey fun.

**O Holy Spirit, flow through me,
I am the open door for thee.
O mighty rushing stream of Light,
transcendence is my sacred right.**

8. Paul the Venetian, help us accept that each of us has a right to be at our present level of consciousness and express our vision. The other partner has a right to respond to this based on his or her level of consciousness.

Master Paul, you balance all,
the seven rays upon my call.
Master Paul, you paint the sky,
with colors that delight the I.

O Holy Spirit, flow through me,
I am the open door for thee.
O mighty rushing stream of Light,
transcendence is my sacred right.

9. Paul the Venetian, help us accept that we do not have a right to react negatively when the other partner exercises free will, because we cannot demand that the other person makes a certain choice.

Master Paul, your Presence here,
filling up my inner sphere.
Life is now a sacred flow,
God Love I do on all bestow.

O Holy Spirit, flow through me,
I am the open door for thee.
O mighty rushing stream of Light,
transcendence is my sacred right.

4. We are open doors for love

1. Paul the Venetian, help us overcome the epic mindset that makes us believe certain outer changes absolutely must happen at a certain time.

> Master Nada, beauty's power,
> unfolding like a sacred flower.
> Master Nada, so sublime,
> a will that conquers even time.
>
> **O Holy Spirit, flow through me,**
> **I am the open door for thee.**
> **O mighty rushing stream of Light,**
> **transcendence is my sacred right.**

2. Paul the Venetian, help us transcend fear-based service in which we become more and more frustrated until we experience a burn-out.

> Master Nada, you bestow,
> upon me wisdom's rushing flow.
> Master Nada, mind so strong
> rising on your wings of song.
>
> **O Holy Spirit, flow through me,**
> **I am the open door for thee.**
> **O mighty rushing stream of Light,**
> **transcendence is my sacred right.**

3. Paul the Venetian, help us be able to take the longer view, be more patient and achieve results over a long period of time.

Master Nada, precious scent,
your love is truly heaven-sent.
Master Nada, kind and soft
on wings of love we rise aloft.

O Holy Spirit, flow through me,
I am the open door for thee.
O mighty rushing stream of Light,
transcendence is my sacred right.

4. Paul the Venetian, help us see that no matter what has happened in our relationship in the past, the opportunity to grow can never be lost.

Master Nada, mother light,
my heart is rising like a kite.
Master Nada, from your view,
all life is pure as morning dew.

O Holy Spirit, flow through me,
I am the open door for thee.
O mighty rushing stream of Light,
transcendence is my sacred right.

5. Paul the Venetian, help us overcome the conflict-creating mindset of "now or never." Help us be true emissaries of peace.

Master Nada, truth you bring,
as morning birds in love do sing.
Master Nada, I now feel,
your love that all four bodies heal.

O Holy Spirit, flow through me,
I am the open door for thee.
O mighty rushing stream of Light,
transcendence is my sacred right.

6. Paul the Venetian, help us see that two people cannot serve each other if each has a vision of how the other person should change and they are both in the all-or-nothing, now-or-never, mentality.

Master Nada, serve in peace,
as all emotions I release.
Master Nada, life is fun,
my solar plexus is a sun.

O Holy Spirit, flow through me,
I am the open door for thee.
O mighty rushing stream of Light,
transcendence is my sacred right.

7. Paul the Venetian, help us see that serving another person is giving the other person an opportunity to grow, not producing a certain outer result. Help us be patient with ourselves and each other.

Master Nada, love is free,
with no conditions binding me.
Master Nada, rise above,
all human forms of lesser love.

O Holy Spirit, flow through me,
I am the open door for thee.
O mighty rushing stream of Light,
transcendence is my sacred right.

8. Paul the Venetian, help us see that nobody has ever attained peace without going through the doorway of patience, which sometimes requires long-suffering.

Master Nada, balance all,
the seven rays upon my call.
Master Nada, rise and shine,
your radiant beauty most divine.

O Holy Spirit, flow through me,
I am the open door for thee.
O mighty rushing stream of Light,
transcendence is my sacred right.

9. Paul the Venetian, help us see that we cannot attain peace as long as we are attached to outer results. Help us accept that we are not the doers; the River of Life is the doer. We provide the chalice and then we let love do its work, being at peace regardless of the physical outcome.

Nada Dear, your Presence here,
filling up my inner sphere.
Life is now a sacred flow,
God Peace on all I do bestow.

O Holy Spirit, flow through me,
I am the open door for thee.
O mighty rushing stream of Light,
transcendence is my sacred right.

Sealing:

In the name of the Divine Mother, I fully accept that the power of these calls is used to set free the Ma-ter light, so it can outpicture the perfect vision of Christ for my own life, for all people and for the planet. In the name I AM THAT I AM, it is done! Amen.

16 | LOVE AND FREEDOM

I AM Paul the Venetian, Chohan of the Third Ray and I am free. I am free because I have overcome all perversions of love.

The concept of free love

When you come to the seventh level at my retreat, I will present you with the opportunity to overcome one of the most prevalent perversions of love on planet earth. It is the concept that became so well-known in the 1960s, that of "free love."

In many cases, free love meant free sex with as many different partners as possible. Do you, perhaps, see that in the 1960s there was also a movement towards giving greater freedom and equality to women? At the same time, there was the promotion of the concept of free love.

What did free love mean in many cases? In the old days when a man would marry the woman he had sex with, then the woman had some protection of being now in a stable relationship. In the free love movement where was the protection for the women? Was it not so that free love was mainly for the men so that they could express their drive to have sex with many different women without any responsibility? Was this liberating women or was it exposing them to a new form of tyranny, the tyranny of being merely a sexual object rather than a life partner?

Strange as it may seem, the free love movement did also have a positive effect, in the sense that the old patterns between the sexes had to be broken up. As I have explained before, things are so bad on planet earth that sometimes drastic methods are needed in order to break up the old. This does not mean that we of the ascended masters condone the methods. It only means we see that, in some cases, nothing else will work. We simply allow people to outplay the tendencies they have in their consciousness, for they will not listen to us anyway. If you will not hear, you must feel, as some of you have probably heard as children. Unfortunately, that is the way it is with many people on earth. They learn only through pain. They do not easily learn from Divine direction.

When you consider the free love movement, you might compare it to a common saying, namely that there are no free lunches. Is there such a thing as free love? You live in a world where everything is energy. Everything you do is done with energy. When you have sex with many different partners, you exchange energy every time. Does that set you free or does it burden you with taking in energy from your sexual partners and depleting your own energy supply? Do you in the long run simply burn yourself out by having free love?

You may look at many people who were part of the most intense experiments in the 1960s and see that, through the combination of sex with many partners and drugs, they did burn themselves out. Their chakras became depleted. They became literally over-stimulated to the point where they could not handle it. The integrity of the chakras, the delicate energetic structures of the chakras, started breaking down.

There are many people who were part of the hippie movement in the 1960s and beyond who have aborted their Divine plans. They depleted their energies to the point where there was neither the energy nor the integrity to carry out what was in their Divine plans. What shall we do with the fact that love on earth is so closely linked to sexual activity?

First of all, we shall realize that we of the ascended masters have ascended. This means we have transcended the consciousness that is so common on earth. We are not afraid to talk about sex. We have no compunctions about talking about this issue or any other issue. Why is it that so many spiritual people, especially ascended master students, especially ascended master students in the United States, cannot talk freely about sex? Why is that, my beloved? It cannot come from the ascended level, can it?

It must be because you are still affected by a particular aspect of the fallen consciousness that wants you to suppress your sexual urges and your sexual energies. They want to make it seem like it is embarrassing to acknowledge that you have a sex drive and that your body has certain hormones and needs. You should not talk about this openly but allow it all to be hush-hush.

This is the old perversion. Do you really think that the intense repression of sexual energy and conversation around sex that were so common until the 1960s was condoned or instituted by the ascended masters? If you do, you are entirely mistaken.

Sexual energies did not cause the fall

Some of you may have heard or read that Jesus intended to free women in his ministry two thousand years ago. I can assure you that Jesus had no compunctions about talking about sex, although it was difficult to do it in the cultural context back then. It was the Catholic Church that really started the suppression of sexual energies and all talk about sex. The Church made it seem like it was sex that was the cause of the fall, which even some ascended master students believe.

How could your sexual energies cause the fall when the fall happened in a previous sphere? People did not have physical bodies with the same characteristics as your bodies have on earth. In those previous spheres, the energies were less dense. There was no need to have physical intercourse in order to produce a child.

How could sexual intercourse have caused the fall? It did not. It was the beings in the fallen consciousness and their rebellion against God and free will that caused the fall. They do not want you to know this so they are attempting to misdirect you into thinking it is all kinds of other things. Saying that it was sexual energy, intercourse, that caused the fall is also a very convenient way to blame women for the fall.

It is a common experience on earth that men have the greater sex drive and that they project out that it is the women who are seducing them. This is the ego's tendency to project that the problem is out there. Women have been blamed for being the ones who seduce the men when the reality is that it is the men who have not been willing to control their sex drive. They have not been able to control it because they have not been able to talk freely about it, due to the culture having been so dysfunctional that it has been a taboo. This is one polarity of the perversion of the fallen consciousness, but the opposite polarity is free love and free sex. Neither polarity will get you to heaven. Neither polarity will get you to heaven on earth.

The difference between sex and love

When you come to the seventh level of my retreat, you had better be ready to talk about sex. You will not pass the initiations at that level unless you are willing to take a look at the topic of sex as it relates to love. Sex is not synonymous with love. It is entirely possible to express love, even between a man and a woman, without having sex. I am not saying it is *common*. I am only saying it is *possible*.

When you grow on the spiritual path, you will first go through a disturbing period where you need to begin to look at some of the things that you have not looked at before. In many cases, they were suppressed in the culture in which you grew up. How many of you grew up in an environment where you could freely talk about sex? Very few. When you come to my retreat, we sit down in a protected environment, in a loving environment, and we take a look at sex and love—and we talk about it. We talk about it until you are able to talk about it freely at the etheric level. I am giving you this teaching in a physical form because I am hoping that you will be able to use it to draw into your conscious mind the initiations you are going through at the etheric level.

Why is it so important to consider the topic of sex? It is extremely important that you learn to express love freely. Because sex has been so synonymous or intertwined with love, it is impossible on this planet to express love freely unless you have looked at and overcome the perversions related to sex. Ideally, you should be able to freely express love towards a person of the opposite sex (or for that matter even the same sex) without stirring up any sexual energies or attraction between you. This is also a necessary step towards having success in relationships.

Sexual attraction and karma

Let us be honest here and acknowledge that you who are on the spiritual path are often moving very fast. You are working through your karma at a much quicker pace than people who are not spiritual and who do not have the tools and the teachings of the ascended masters. In the old days, in your parents' generation, it was common that a man and a woman would be attracted to each other and would end up marrying because they had karma to balance with each other. In many cases, it would take people a lifetime to balance the karma. With the tools and the teachings of the ascended masters, if you are in a karmic relationship, you can often balance that karma very quickly. Any relationship you engage in on earth has some karma involved with it. It is almost impossible to engage in a relationship on earth without having karma with the other person.

What happens if you are attracted to a person because you have some karma to balance with that person? You get married and you have children. After a few years, the newness of the relationship has worn off. You also have the daily humdrum of the routine with the kids and work and this and that, and suddenly the newness and the attraction is not there. Maybe you have even balanced the karma that drew you together. Now, one of you (or both of you) meets another person and you feel you have karma with that person. This often results in a sexual attraction.

Are you then supposed to leave the previous relationship, abandon your children, with all the ramifications this has for how children are affected by a divorce, so that you can go with this other person? Are you supposed to have children with that person, and again after a few years, the karma has been balanced, the newness has worn off and now there is another person you are attracted to? You can go on like this throughout your life, and how many families can one person start in a lifetime? How many families can one person leave behind in a lifetime without it wearing on you?

The golden age model for families is that people grow to the maximum extent possible. Growth is always the primary goal. It is not necessarily a golden age model that every marriage should last either for a lifetime or untill the children have grown. There can be situations where it is constructive for the growth of both partners that you break up a marriage, even if children are involved. The golden age model is that most people would not do this because they would engage in a relationship from a greater level of maturity. They would decide to have children only when they are making a commitment to raising those children together, giving them a stable environment. This is not an environment like what you saw in the old days where people would stay together, but an environment that is dynamic because there is still growth.

How can this be achieved? It can be achieved if you have a clear commitment that you are in a relationship and you have committed to raising the children in that relationship. What happens if, after a few years, you meet a person of the opposite sex and you feel an attraction to that person? You have karma with that person. How can you balance that karma? You *can* if you can disassociate love from sex. Then you can have a loving relationship and express genuine love towards that person without having to have the sexual interaction, which raises certain complications. This means you can now have a loving relationship with this person while preserving your marriage because there is no infidelity and your partner does not feel threatened.

The energetic ties in sexual relationships

At the same time, you can work out the karma with the new person without having a sexual relationship with that person. You can actually grow much faster than what you see right now where people are attracted to a person for karmic reasons and it ends up in a sexual relationship and maybe it produces children. All of a sudden, there are so many energetic ties that it becomes a strain to break them up.

Establishing a relationship is establishing a set of very complex energetic ties between two people. They become even more complex when children are involved. Breaking up this will always be a certain strain on you, at least energetically. With the negative feelings that are often involved, it becomes an even greater strain. When you establish a new relationship, this also becomes a strain, especially in today's age where your partner may have children from a previous relationship and you do as well. Now, there is a whole different set of complications that come into the interaction. I am not saying anything about right and wrong here. I am just explaining to you the complications that are involved at an energy level. In the golden age it is necessary, especially for the spiritual people, to find a way whereby you can balance karma, or fulfill a certain relationship with another person, without going into the complexity of having a sexual relationship with a possible production of children and so forth and so on.

Love without sex

You can make much faster progress this way, and this means that you must be able to have a relationship with a person of the opposite sex, or even of the same sex, without thinking that love can only be expressed through sex. You need to find a way to express genuine love, which is the fastest way to balance karma, without going into the complications of a sexual relationship that so often causes the old relationship to break up.

I know that some people who are considering themselves to be very progressive are saying: "But does that not mean we should strive for an ideal where, even though you are in a committed relationship and raising children, you can still have other sexual partners as you feel you need to?" I am not saying that this cannot be done, but I am saying that it is very difficult to do this, especially in the current conditions on earth.

Something does happen when you cross the line to having a physical, sexual relationship. There is a closer involvement. It is possible to not have these ramifications, but it is very difficult to have it in an environment like earth. If you are a practical realist, you will recognize that you can make much faster progress if you do not have to have a sexual relationship with every person with whom you have karma to balance in this lifetime.

Balancing the karma in a sexual relationship

You do understand, do you not, that if you have karma with a person of the opposite sex, then balancing that karma cannot be done by either ignoring the relationship or by locking it in a pattern where you are so distant that you are only being polite with each other? In order to balance the karma, it is often necessary that two people come together and openly discuss why they feel an attraction. This may necessitate that they have deeper, more personal conversations and that they express love towards each other freely without making it physical, at least not sexual. This is the fastest way to balance the karma and work through that relationship.

I am not saying here that you should *not* have several relationships in your lifetime, but you do all realize that there is a limit to how many relationships you can have. There is a cost in having many different relationships, especially sexual relationships. Most of the people who have had many sexual partners have both depleted their own energy and have received energy from their partners that is burdening them. That is why I am saying that if you can find a way to express love without making it sexual, you can balance the karma and make much faster progress. You cannot do this if every attraction to a person of the opposite sex has to be carried through a physical, sexual relationship. This is a higher way to have free love that is not free sex.

What do you want: maximum growth or maximum pleasure? We recognize that given the suppression of sexual energies that has been going on for over 1700 years in the Christian culture, there is a need for a period where people have a more free view of sex so that they can work through their repression. For some people, this does necessitate that they have several partners in a lifetime or that they have partners where the main focus of the relationship is sex.

We are not necessarily against you working through your sexual repression and your sexual desires. Sometimes we even do what Jesus did when he said to Judas: "Whatever thou doest, do quickly." If there is something you have to work through, then work through it so you can get on with your Divine plan, or at least with other aspects of your Divine plan. Working through your issues is certainly part of your Divine plan, but perhaps not the more important part of the service you can give to the world.

If you have, for many lifetimes, been in a culture where you had to suppress your sexual desires and energies, then it can be necessary for you to rise above that, to work through it. If you can find a partner who has the same desire, and you can both be conscious of the fact that you are simply helping each other work through this, then this may be a way to growth. I strongly encourage you to work through your sexual drive and desires with the fewest number of partners. The more partners you have, the more costly it becomes energetically. This is simply the way things are, given the current conditions on earth.

A more natural view of love and sex

What we do at my retreat is to help you overcome the illusion of free love and the illusion that sex should be suppressed. We help you have a natural view of sex and a natural view of love. How can you have a natural view of love if you think love has to be expressed through sex? Consider that there is such a heavy burden of an unnatural view of sex on this planet that you can hardly have a natural view of love if you think that love and sex have to be linked. The first step is to disassociate love and sex from each other. Then you can build a more natural view of love, and you can use that to build a more natural view of sex. You are liberated from the unnatural view of both love and sex. Naturally, sexuality is a complex topic. It is not my intent here to give you a complete discourse on it. I am only stirring up in your conscious mind some of the things that we deal with at the seventh level of my retreat.

The goal at my retreat is to help you express love more freely. The plan of my retreat is that you work through the perversions of love that are found on this planet so that you become able to freely express your love. You can express it through any relationship you have. You can express love freely to your children, to your parents, to your coworkers, to your friends, to your spouse.

There is a great need for people who are free to express love in whatever form is appropriate, based on the physical nature of the relationship. There is a great need for people who can tell the difference between what is appropriate and not appropriate, not according to the old standard of sexual repression but according to the higher view of what promotes growth.

The Alpha and Omega flow of love

We desire all those who pass through our retreat of the Third Ray to make significant progress towards being able to freely express love. Once you have started to overcome the hurdle of *expressing* love, you also need to work on the Omega aspect of *receiving* love. What good does it do you to express your love if the other person in the relationship cannot receive love? How can you help another person more freely express love to you if you cannot receive love from that person?

Alpha and Omega in a free-flowing polarity give rise to new life—that is the creative force and how it works. That is what has built the entire world of form. The interplay of the Alpha and the Omega in a free flow of love gives rise to new life, new forms, new expressions, new finite expressions of the infinite Spirit. Because they are free expressions, they are not locked in a pattern. They are free to flow on to become more. They are part of the River of Life, they are part of the driving force that causes the entire River to become more in this constant dance of God.

For love to be expressed, it must be allowed to flow. You do not own love, you do not produce it, you can only let it flow through you. The more you can be an open door for love (the more freely you can let it express itself through you), the more love will come into this world through your chakras and your soul vehicle. It is not the soul vehicle, not even your chakras, that are the open door for love. It is the Conscious You, and the more the Conscious You can be conscious of itself as pure awareness, as the open door, the more love will flow through you into the chakras and the soul vehicle. Once in the chakras and the soul vehicle, it will find expression in the world. In order for it to find free expression, your chakras and your soul vehicle must be as free as possible from the many perversions that restrict, suppress or misdirect the flow of love.

In the old days, the suppression of sexual energies restricted the free flow of love. The free love movement opened up for a flow, but it was misdirected into sexual energies. It was not actually love that was being expressed, but only the lower desires of the physical body, which are close to the animalistic desires.

Expressing your sexual drive responsibly

If you look at animals, you will see that they have a sexual drive, but there are hardly any animals that have sex as much as human beings do. This is partly because human beings have a higher level of consciousness so they are not living in order to fulfill animalistic drives, such as propagation. Human beings can enjoy any activity, including sex, and there is not anything wrong with enjoying it. In order to continue to enjoy it, you need to recognize that if the animalistic desire for physical sex is unhooked from the need for propagation, then there is nothing that restricts it at the physical level.

That is when you have sex addiction, people who can never get enough sex and who feel incomplete unless they are close to or in a state of orgasm, which you cannot be all the time. You need to realize that, when the physical body and the need for propagation is not restricting the sex drive, then the higher mind needs to restrict it so that you find a balance where you can actually function. You may think that the people who are addicted to sex are enjoying it, but they are not enjoying it. They have a compulsory drive to have it, and most of the time they are either not enjoying it because they are not having sex or they are not enjoying it while they are having sex because what is going to happen afterwards when they feel empty again? How are they going to get the next fix?

There is a legitimate goal to establish for yourself as a spiritual person. It is to come to the point where you can express your sexual drive in a responsible manner that does not hinder your growth and does not take your energies into a lower level or deplete your energies. You have a partner who also has a certain level of maturity and freedom, and you can have sex and fully enjoy it, not from an animalistic point of enjoyment, but from a higher enjoyment that comes from feeling the closeness, even a sense of oneness, with another person.

A higher form of oneness

You will know that teachers in the East, such as Padma Sambhava, practiced tantric sex. I am not encouraging this in this discourse because this is a much bigger topic. I am only using it to show ascended master students that suppressing the sex drive is not necessarily the only or the highest way to spiritual growth. You can free this desire to the point where you can express it in a balanced way that is not only enjoyable in a higher sense but also helps you establish a closeness, or oneness, with another human being. This can be a step towards stepping outside of your soul vehicle and reestablishing the awareness of yourself as connected to something greater than yourself and as being pure awareness.

The highest form of sexual intercourse can be achieved only when both partners have a high degree of awareness that they are the Conscious You and that they are pure awareness. If you help each other step out of your normal state of consciousness and you both experience sexual intercourse as a state of pure awareness, then you achieve the goal that is the goal of tantric sex. It is *not* to have the most intense possible orgasm. It is to have the highest degree of oneness through the purity of awareness where the borderline between you and your partner begins to break down and the Conscious You of one person flows into the Conscious You of the other. You now form a polarity that is the higher creative polarity.

When two ascended masters come together in order to attain a certain purpose, we merge our beings. We are not having sexual intercourse, but we are merging our beings. It is through this merging, where we form a polarity of Alpha and Omega, that we create a new form, a new result, a new energetic impulse. This is how it works in the spiritual realm. You cannot completely copy this in the physical, but you can strive for some degree of it. It can be achieved *through* sexual intercourse. It can also be achieved *without* sexual intercourse.

I am giving you a higher vision of what confuses some of you, namely why certain people, who are now ascended masters, practiced tantric sex. Tantric sex has been perverted as everything else. It has been turned into this drive for a physical result.

If you can disassociate it from that and seek oneness through a free flow, an expression of love, then it can be a tool to enhance spiritual growth and sexual freedom. Does that mean that all ascended master students need to have or practice tantric sex? Of course not.

It can also be achieved in other ways, and that is why we have given you the path of self-mastery where we use teachings and the invocation of light to bring you towards that same result. I naturally recommend that you follow this course, but I do want to make you aware in the outer what we discuss at the etheric level of my retreat. You need to be aware of the different aspects of love and sexuality in order to free yourself from the many dysfunctional aspects that are floating around in the collective consciousness, seeking to use especially sexuality but also love to abort or misdirect your spiritual growth.

Only those who know will be able to be free. Knowledge is not only power, it is also the key to freedom. You are not free by simply escaping a certain activity. You are free only by knowing the illusion that gave rise to that activity and then choosing freely and knowingly to transcend it. *That* is freedom, *knowing* freedom.

Graduating from the Third Ray

It is my desire at my retreat to bring you to the point where you have achieved knowing freedom concerning love. I can now take you to the graduation ceremony in my retreat where I can take you into a special room. This is a room where you will be seated on a very comfortable chair, almost like a throne.

As you sit there, you will experience that the room opens up. There are no walls, but you see the vastness of the physical universe. Then you see beyond it and see the vastness of the cosmos with other spheres. This is my parting gift to you, this sense of infinity, the infinity of love that freely flows through all levels of the cosmos. I allow you to be immersed in this experience for as long as you desire, but there will come a point where you naturally begin to come out of it and again become aware of yourself and your soul vehicle here on earth. That is the moment where I can put my arm around your shoulder and lead you out of the door into a room where there is an intense white light. The white light is produced by my beloved brother and fellow Chohan, Serapis Bey, who is waiting to take you to the next level of initiations at his retreat.

Here you might witness something that gives us, the Chohans, intense joy. What is my greatest joy as a Chohan? It is to have taken a student through all levels of initiation at my retreat. When do I feel this joy fulfilled? I feel it when I pass you on to the next Chohan. When I present you to Serapis, there is a moment where we look each other in the eye, and we merge in that highest state of oneness that you have at the ascended level. Nothing is said with worldly words, but a world is said beyond words. Serapis feels my joy, and he reciprocates with his joy of receiving you as his student. *His* greatest joy is to take you through the levels of initiation at his retreat, but he cannot even begin this until you are ready because you have passed the initiations at my retreat.

There is that moment where we share this infinite joy. If you pay attention, you may catch a glimpse of it and feel the joy of you knowing that you are the cause of our joy. This may give you an impetus to move onward. I can assure you that you need that impetus in order to pass the somewhat more intense initiations under Serapis. Of course, I do not wish to in any way give you a hint of what awaits you, for surely the initiations of the Fourth Ray are best enjoyed when one does not know what is coming.

I tease you in the end, but so far I have not expressed much humor. I can assure you that I do so at the retreat. It is just so difficult to express humor in a book because humor is such a conflict-producing topic on earth. We generally prefer to avoid it in books that can be read by people from many cultural backgrounds. I assure you that at the retreats, we can somewhat rise above this, and we do actually have much more fun than you would ever suspect from reading the physical book.

I sincerely hope that this expression of my love for you in a physical form has served to inspire you to bring into the physical that which you have already learned at the etheric level of my retreat. I know well that it is possible that people can find and read this book without actually following the initiations at inner levels. Anyone can read it as an intellectual exercise, or they can read it for the purpose of just putting it down. I would suggest that few people who have these intentions would make it to the end. Even if they do, they have received an opportunity to choose love. Should they decide *not* to choose love, then I still know that I have fulfilled my purpose for bringing forth this book.

I have presented the opportunity to choose love. I am content with giving you complete freedom of choice, for I have complete freedom of love, flowing with love and expressing my love.

Paul the Venetian I AM. I am an ascended master. I am the Chohan of the Third Ray of infinite, unbound, incomparable, unconditional love.

LOVE

17 | I INVOKE FREEDOM TO LOVE

In the name I AM THAT I AM, Jesus Christ, I call to my I AM Presence to flow through the I Will Be Presence that I AM and give this invocation with full power. I call to beloved Elohim Heros and Amora and Arcturus and Victoria, Archangel Chamuel and Charity and Zadkiel and Amethyst, Paul the Venetian and Saint Germain to help us give and receive love freely. Help us see and surrender all patterns that block our oneness with Paul the Venetian and with our I AM Presences, including …

[Make personal calls]

1. We have balanced sexuality

1. Paul the Venetian, help us overcome the illusions of free love and free sex.

> O Heros-Amora, in your love so pink,
> I care not what others about me may think,
> in oneness with you, I claim a new day,
> an innocent child, I frolic and play.

O Heros-Amora, a new life begun,
I laugh at the devil, the serious one,
I bathe in your glorious Ruby-Pink Sun,
knowing my God allows life to be fun.

2. Paul the Venetian, help us overcome the old patterns between the sexes without turning women into sexual objects instead of long-term partners.

O Heros-Amora, life is such a joy,
I see that the world is like a great toy,
whatever my mind into it projects,
the mirror of life exactly reflects.

O Heros-Amora, I reap what I sow,
yet this is Plan B for helping me grow,
for truly, Plan A is that I join the flow,
immersed in the Infinite Love you bestow.

3. Paul the Venetian, help us find a balance where we can express our sexuality without burning out our chakras.

O Heros-Amora, conditions you burn,
I know I AM free to take a new turn,
Immersed in the stream of infinite Love,
I know that my Spirit came from Above.

O Heros-Amora, awakened I see,
in true love is no conditionality,
the devil is stuck in his duality,
but I AM set free by Love's reality.

4. Paul the Venetian, help us find a balanced sexuality so we do not deplete our energies but have the energy and the integrity to fulfill our Divine plans.

O Heros-Amora, I feel that at last,
I've risen above the trap of my past,
in true love I claim my freedom to grow,
forever I'm one with Love's Infinite Flow.

O Heros-Amora, conditions are ties,
forming a net of serpentine lies,
your love has no bounds, forever it flies,
raising all life into Ruby-Pink skies.

5. Paul the Venetian, help us talk freely about sex and transcend the particular aspect of the fallen consciousness that wants us to suppress our sexual urges and our sexual energies.

Beloved Arcturus, release now the flow,
of Violet Flame to help all life grow,
in ever-expanding circles of Light,
it pulses within every atom so bright.

Beloved Arcturus, thou Elohim Free,
I open my heart to your reality,
expanding my heart into Infinity,
your flame is the key to my God-victory.

6. Paul the Venetian, help us overcome the illusion that sex was the cause of the fall.

Beloved Arcturus, be with me alway,
reborn, I am ready to face a new day,
I have no attachments to life here on earth,
I claim a new life in your Flame of Rebirth.

Beloved Arcturus, your Violet Flame pure,
is for every ailment the ultimate cure,
against it no darkness could ever endure,
my freedom it will forever ensure.

7. Paul the Venetian, help us overcome both perversions of the fallen consciousness, namely the suppression of sex and free sex.

Beloved Arcturus, your bright violet fire,
now fills every atom, raising them higher,
the space in each atom all filled with your light,
as matter itself is shining so bright.

Beloved Arcturus, your transforming Grace,
empowers me now every challenge to face,
as your violet light floods my inner space,
towards my ascension I willingly race.

8. Paul the Venetian, help us understand that sex is not synonymous with love and that it is possible to express love between a man and a woman without having sex.

Beloved Arcturus, bring in a new age,
help earth and humanity turn a new page,
your transforming light gives me certainty,
Saint Germain's Golden Age is a reality.

Beloved Arcturus, I surrender all fear,
I AM feeling your Presence so tangibly near,
with your Freedom's Song filling my ear,
I know that to God I AM ever so dear.

9. Paul the Venetian, help us learn to express love freely. Help us see that it is impossible to express love freely unless we have looked at and overcome the perversions related to sex.

Accelerate into Oneness, I AM real,
Accelerate into Oneness, all life heal,
Accelerate into Oneness, I AM MORE,
Accelerate into Oneness, all will soar.

Accelerate into Oneness! (3X)
Beloved Heros and Amora.
Accelerate into Oneness! (3X)
Beloved Chamuel and Charity.
Accelerate into Oneness! (3X)
Beloved Paul the Venetian.
Accelerate into Oneness! (3X)
Beloved I AM.

2. We can separate love and sexuality

1. Paul the Venetian, help us learn to express love towards another person without stirring up any sexual energies or attraction between ourselves and other people.

Chamuel Archangel, in ruby ray power,
I know I am taking a life-giving shower.
Love burning away all perversions of will,
I suddenly feel my desires falling still.

Chamuel Archangel, descend from Above,
Chamuel Archangel, with ruby-pink love,
Chamuel Archangel, so often thought-of,
Chamuel Archangel, o come Holy Dove.

2. Paul the Venetian, help us see that we are often sexually attracted to a person because we have karma with that person.

Chamuel Archangel, a spiral of light,
as ruby ray fire now pierces the night.
All forces of darkness consumed by your fire,
consuming all those who will not rise higher.

Chamuel Archangel, descend from Above,
Chamuel Archangel, with ruby-pink love,
Chamuel Archangel, so often thought-of,
Chamuel Archangel, o come Holy Dove.

3. Paul the Venetian, help us see how we can balance the karma with other people without entering a sexual or physical relationship or breaking up an existing relationship.

Chamuel Archangel, your love so immense,
with clarified vision, my life now makes sense.
The purpose of life you so clearly reveal,
immersed in your love, God's oneness I feel.

Chamuel Archangel, descend from Above,
Chamuel Archangel, with ruby-pink love,
Chamuel Archangel, so often thought-of,
Chamuel Archangel, o come Holy Dove.

4. Paul the Venetian, help us tune in to the golden age matrix for relationships so we can see how to have both stability and growth in our relationship.

Chamuel Archangel, what calmness you bring,
I see now that even death has no sting.
For truly, in love there can be no decay,
as love is transcendence into a new day.

Chamuel Archangel, descend from Above,
Chamuel Archangel, with ruby-pink love,
Chamuel Archangel, so often thought-of,
Chamuel Archangel, o come Holy Dove.

5. Paul the Venetian, help us disassociate love from sex so we can have loving relationships with other people without going into a sexual relationship with the complications that involves.

Zadkiel Archangel, your flow is so swift,
in your violet light, I instantly shift,
into a vibration in which I am free,
from all limitations of the lesser me.

Zadkiel Archangel, encircle the earth,
Zadkiel Archangel, with your violet girth,
Zadkiel Archangel, unstoppable mirth,
Zadkiel Archangel, our planet's rebirth.

6. Paul the Venetian, help us learn how to balance karma with another person without having a sexual relationship, thereby growing much faster.

Zadkiel Archangel, I truly aspire,
to being the master of your violet fire.
Wielding the power, of your alchemy,
I use Sacred Word, to set all life free.

Zadkiel Archangel, encircle the earth,
Zadkiel Archangel, with your violet girth,
Zadkiel Archangel, unstoppable mirth,
Zadkiel Archangel, our planet's rebirth.

7. Paul the Venetian, help us find a way to express genuine love towards other people, which is the fastest way to balance karma, without going into the complications of a sexual relationship.

Zadkiel Archangel, your violet light,
transforming the earth, with unstoppable might.
So swiftly our planet, beginning to spin,
with legions of angels, our victory we win.

Zadkiel Archangel, encircle the earth,
Zadkiel Archangel, with your violet girth,
Zadkiel Archangel, unstoppable mirth,
Zadkiel Archangel, our planet's rebirth.

8. Paul the Venetian, help us work through our sexual repressions from this or past lifetimes without depleting our energies or taking focus away from our Divine plans.

Zadkiel Archangel, your violet flame,
the earth and humanity, never the same.
Saint Germain's Golden Age, is a reality,
what glorious wonder, I joyously see.

Zadkiel Archangel, encircle the earth,
Zadkiel Archangel, with your violet girth,
Zadkiel Archangel, unstoppable mirth,
Zadkiel Archangel, our planet's rebirth.

9. Paul the Venetian, help us have a natural view of sex and a natural view of love. Help us disassociate love and sex from each other. Help us build a more natural view of love that leads to a more natural view of sex.

With angels I soar,
as I reach for MORE.
The angels so real,
their love all will heal.
The angels bring peace,
all conflicts will cease.
With angels of light,
we soar to new height.

The rustling sound of angel wings,
what joy as even matter sings,
what joy as every atom rings,
in harmony with angel wings.

3. We are free to express love

1. Paul the Venetian, help us be free to express love towards other people in whatever form is appropriate, based on the physical nature of the relationship.

Master Paul, venetian dream,
your love for beauty's flowing stream.
Master Paul, in love's own womb,
your power shatters ego's tomb.

O Holy Spirit, flow through me,
I am the open door for thee.
O mighty rushing stream of Light,
transcendence is my sacred right.

2. Paul the Venetian, help us know the difference between what is appropriate and not appropriate, not according to the old standard of sexual repression but according to the higher view of what promotes growth.

Master Paul, your counsel wise,
my mind is raised to lofty skies.
Master Paul, in wisdom's love,
such beauty flowing from Above.

O Holy Spirit, flow through me,
I am the open door for thee.
O mighty rushing stream of Light,
transcendence is my sacred right.

3. Paul the Venetian, help us overcome all limitations to receiving love from each other and other people.

Master Paul, love is an art,
it opens up the secret heart.
Master Paul, love's rushing flow,
my heart awash in sacred glow.

O Holy Spirit, flow through me,
I am the open door for thee.
O mighty rushing stream of Light,
transcendence is my sacred right.

4. Paul the Venetian, help us grasp that the interplay of the Alpha and the Omega in a free flow of love gives rise to new life, new forms, new expressions, new finite expressions of the infinite Spirit.

Master Paul, accelerate,
upon pure love I meditate.
Master Paul, intentions pure,
my self-transcendence will ensure.

O Holy Spirit, flow through me,
I am the open door for thee.
O mighty rushing stream of Light,
transcendence is my sacred right.

5. Paul the Venetian, help us grasp that for love to be expressed, it must be allowed to flow. We do not own love, we do not produce it, we can only let it flow through us.

Master Paul, your love will heal,
my inner light you do reveal.
Master Paul, all life console,
with you I'm being truly whole.

O Holy Spirit, flow through me,
I am the open door for thee.
O mighty rushing stream of Light,
transcendence is my sacred right.

6. Paul the Venetian, help us grasp that the more we can be an open door for love, the more freely we can let it express itself through us, the more love will come into this world through our chakras and our soul vehicles.

Master Paul, you serve the All,
by helping us transcend the fall.
Master Paul, in peace we rise,
as ego meets its sure demise.

O Holy Spirit, flow through me,
I am the open door for thee.
O mighty rushing stream of Light,
transcendence is my sacred right.

7. Paul the Venetian, help us grasp that the open door for love is the Conscious You. The more the Conscious You can be conscious of itself as pure awareness, the more love will flow through us into the chakras and the soul vehicle.

Master Paul, love all life free,
your love is for eternity.
Master Paul, you are the One,
to help us make the journey fun.

O Holy Spirit, flow through me,
I am the open door for thee.
O mighty rushing stream of Light,
transcendence is my sacred right.

8. Paul the Venetian, help us grasp that while there is nothing wrong with enjoying sex, we need to express our sexual drive in a manner that does not hinder our growth by depleting our energies.

Master Paul, you balance all,
the seven rays upon my call.
Master Paul, you paint the sky,
with colors that delight the I.

O Holy Spirit, flow through me,
I am the open door for thee.
O mighty rushing stream of Light,
transcendence is my sacred right.

9. Paul the Venetian, help us enjoy sex from a higher enjoyment that comes from feeling the closeness, even a sense of oneness, with each other.

Master Paul, your Presence here,
filling up my inner sphere.
Life is now a sacred flow,
God Love I do on all bestow.

O Holy Spirit, flow through me,
I am the open door for thee.
O mighty rushing stream of Light,
transcendence is my sacred right.

4. We knowingly choose freedom

1. Paul the Venetian, help us see that establishing closeness, or oneness, with another human being can be a step towards reestablishing the awareness of ourselves as connected to something greater in pure awareness.

Saint Germain, your alchemy,
with violet fire now sets me free.
Saint Germain, I ever grow,
in freedom's overpowering flow.

O Holy Spirit, flow through me,
I am the open door for thee.
O mighty rushing stream of Light,
transcendence is my sacred right.

2. Paul the Venetian, help us have the highest degree of oneness through the purity of awareness, where the borderline between us breaks down and we form a higher, creative polarity.

Saint Germain, your mastery,
of violet flame geometry.
Saint Germain, in you I see,
the formulas that set me free.

O Holy Spirit, flow through me,
I am the open door for thee.
O mighty rushing stream of Light,
transcendence is my sacred right.

3. Paul the Venetian, help us free ourselves from the many dysfunctional ideas that are seeking to use sexuality and love to abort or misdirect our spiritual growth.

Saint Germain, in Liberty,
I feel the love you have for me.
Saint Germain, I do adore,
the violet flame that makes all more.

O Holy Spirit, flow through me,
I am the open door for thee.
O mighty rushing stream of Light,
transcendence is my sacred right.

4. Paul the Venetian, help us grasp that knowledge is the key to freedom. We are free only by knowing the illusion that gave rise to a certain activity and freely choosing to transcend it.

Saint Germain, in unity,
I will transcend duality.
Saint Germain, my self so pure,
your violet chemistry so sure.

O Holy Spirit, flow through me,
I am the open door for thee.
O mighty rushing stream of Light,
transcendence is my sacred right.

5. Paul the Venetian, help us achieve knowing freedom concerning sexuality so that we can express love freely without having our Divine plans be diverted by sexual attractions.

Saint Germain, reality,
in violet light I am carefree.
Saint Germain, my aura seal,
your violet flame my chakras heal.

O Holy Spirit, flow through me,
I am the open door for thee.
O mighty rushing stream of Light,
transcendence is my sacred right.

6. Paul the Venetian, help us achieve knowing freedom concerning love so that we can allow it to flow through us freely.

Saint Germain, your chemistry,
with violet fire set atoms free.
Saint Germain, from lead to gold,
transforming vision I behold.

O Holy Spirit, flow through me,
I am the open door for thee.
O mighty rushing stream of Light,
transcendence is my sacred right.

7. Paul the Venetian, help us be free to experience the sense of infinity, the infinity of love that freely flows through all levels of the cosmos.

Saint Germain, transcendency,
as I am always one with thee.
Saint Germain, from soul I'm free,
I so delight in being me.

O Holy Spirit, flow through me,
I am the open door for thee.
O mighty rushing stream of Light,
transcendence is my sacred right.

8. Paul the Venetian, help us bring into our conscious awareness everything we have learned at your etheric retreat so that we can put it into practice in all of our relationships.

Saint Germain, nobility,
the key to sacred alchemy.
Saint Germain, you balance all,
the seven rays upon my call.

O Holy Spirit, flow through me,
I am the open door for thee.
O mighty rushing stream of Light,
transcendence is my sacred right.

9. Paul the Venetian, help us have complete freedom of love, flowing with love, both receiving and expressing the infinite, unbound, incomparable and unconditional love of the Third Ray.

Saint Germain, your Presence here,
filling up my inner sphere.
Life is now a sacred flow,
God Freedom I on all bestow.

O Holy Spirit, flow through me,
I am the open door for thee.
O mighty rushing stream of Light,
transcendence is my sacred right.

Sealing:

In the name of the Divine Mother, I fully accept that the power of these calls is used to set free the Ma-ter light, so it can outpicture the perfect vision of Christ for my own life, for all people and for the planet. In the name I AM THAT I AM, it is done! Amen.

3.01 DECREE TO HEROS AND AMORA

In the name I AM THAT I AM, Jesus Christ, I call to my I Will Be Presence to flow through my being and give these decrees with full power. I call to beloved Heros and Amora to release flood tides of Love's Ruby-Pink Fire, to consume in me all conditions that separate me from the River of Life, including… [Make personal calls]

1. O Heros-Amora, in your love so pink,
I care not what others about me may think,
in oneness with you, I claim a new day,
an innocent child, I frolic and play.

O Heros-Amora, a new life begun,
I laugh at the devil, the serious one,
I bathe in your glorious Ruby-Pink Sun,
knowing my God allows life to be fun.

2. O Heros-Amora, life is such a joy,
I see that the world is like a great toy,
whatever my mind into it projects,
the mirror of life exactly reflects.

O Heros-Amora, I reap what I sow,
yet this is Plan B for helping me grow,
for truly, Plan A is that I join the flow,
immersed in the Infinite Love you bestow.

3. O Heros-Amora, conditions you burn,
I know I AM free to take a new turn,
Immersed in the stream of infinite Love,
I know that my Spirit came from Above.

O Heros-Amora, awakened I see,
in true love is no conditionality,
the devil is stuck in his duality,
but I AM set free by Love's reality.

4. O Heros-Amora, I feel that at last,
I've risen above the trap of my past,
in true love I claim my freedom to grow,
forever I'm one with Love's Infinite Flow.

O Heros-Amora, conditions are ties,
forming a net of serpentine lies,
your love has no bounds, forever it flies,
raising all life into Ruby-Pink skies.

Coda:

Accelerate into Oneness, I AM real,
Accelerate into Oneness, all life heal,
Accelerate into Oneness, I AM MORE,
Accelerate into Oneness, all will soar.

Accelerate into Oneness! (3X)
Beloved Heros and Amora.

Accelerate into Oneness! (3X)
Beloved Chamuel and Charity.

Accelerate into Oneness! (3X)
Beloved Paul the Venetian.

Accelerate into Oneness! (3X)
Beloved I AM.

Sealing:

In the name of the Divine Mother, I fully accept that the power of these calls is used to set free the Ma-ter light, so it can outpicture the perfect vision of Christ for my own life, for all people and for the planet. In the name I AM THAT I AM, it is done! Amen.

LOVE

3.02 DECREE TO ARCHANGEL CHAMUEL

In the name I AM THAT I AM, Jesus Christ, I call to my I AM Presence to flow through the I Will Be Presence that I AM and give these decrees with full power. I call to beloved Archangel Chamuel and Charity to shield me in your wings of ruby pink light, and shatter and consume all imperfect energies and dark forces, including... [Make personal calls]

1. Chamuel Archangel, in ruby ray power,
I know I am taking a life-giving shower.
Love burning away all perversions of will,
I suddenly feel my desires falling still

Chamuel Archangel, descend from Above,
Chamuel Archangel, with ruby-pink love,
Chamuel Archangel, so often thought-of,
Chamuel Archangel, o come Holy Dove.

2. Chamuel Archangel, a spiral of light,
as ruby ray fire now pierces the night.
All forces of darkness consumed by your fire,
consuming all those who will not rise higher.

Chamuel Archangel, descend from Above,
Chamuel Archangel, with ruby-pink love,
Chamuel Archangel, so often thought-of,
Chamuel Archangel, o come Holy Dove.

3. Chamuel Archangel, your love so immense,
with clarified vision, my life now makes sense.
The purpose of life you so clearly reveal,
immersed in your love, God's oneness I feel.

Chamuel Archangel, descend from Above,
Chamuel Archangel, with ruby-pink love,
Chamuel Archangel, so often thought-of,
Chamuel Archangel, o come Holy Dove.

4. Chamuel Archangel, what calmness you bring,
I see now that even death has no sting.
For truly, in love there can be no decay,
as love is transcendence into a new day.

Chamuel Archangel, descend from Above,
Chamuel Archangel, with ruby-pink love,
Chamuel Archangel, so often thought-of,
Chamuel Archangel, o come Holy Dove.

Coda:

With angels I soar,
as I reach for MORE.
The angels so real,
their love all will heal.
The angels bring peace,
all conflicts will cease.
With angels of light,
we soar to new height.

The rustling sound of angel wings,
what joy as even matter sings,
what joy as every atom rings,
in harmony with angel wings.

Sealing:

In the name of the Divine Mother, I fully accept that the power of these calls is used to set free the Ma-ter light, so it can outpicture the perfect vision of Christ for my own life, for all people and for the planet. In the name I AM THAT I AM, it is done! Amen.

LOVE

3.03 DECREE TO PAUL THE VENETIAN

In the name I AM THAT I AM, Jesus Christ, I call to my I AM Presence to flow through the I Will Be Presence that I AM and give these decrees with full power. I call to beloved Paul the Venetian, the other Chohans and the Maha Chohan to release flood tides of light, to consume all blocks and attachments that prevent me from becoming one with the eternal flow of the third ray of creative love and ever-transcending oneness, including…

[Make personal calls]

1. Master Paul, venetian dream,
your love for beauty's flowing stream.
Master Paul, in love's own womb,
your power shatters ego's tomb.

O Holy Spirit, flow through me,
I am the open door for thee.
O mighty rushing stream of Light,
transcendence is my sacred right.

2. Master Paul, your counsel wise,
my mind is raised to lofty skies.
Master Paul, in wisdom's love,
such beauty flowing from Above.

O Holy Spirit, flow through me,
I am the open door for thee.
O mighty rushing stream of Light,
transcendence is my sacred right.

3. Master Paul, love is an art,
it opens up the secret heart.
Master Paul, love's rushing flow,
my heart awash in sacred glow.

O Holy Spirit, flow through me,
I am the open door for thee.
O mighty rushing stream of Light,
transcendence is my sacred right.

4. Master Paul, accelerate,
upon pure love I meditate.
Master Paul, intentions pure,
my self-transcendence will ensure.

O Holy Spirit, flow through me,
I am the open door for thee.
O mighty rushing stream of Light,
transcendence is my sacred right.

5. Master Paul, your love will heal,
my inner light you do reveal.
Master Paul, all life console,
with you I'm being truly whole.

O Holy Spirit, flow through me,
I am the open door for thee.
O mighty rushing stream of Light,
transcendence is my sacred right.

6. Master Paul, you serve the All,
by helping us transcend the fall.
Master Paul, in peace we rise,
as ego meets its sure demise.

O Holy Spirit, flow through me,
I am the open door for thee.
O mighty rushing stream of Light,
transcendence is my sacred right.

7. Master Paul, love all life free,
your love is for eternity.
Master Paul, you are the One,
to help us make the journey fun.

O Holy Spirit, flow through me,
I am the open door for thee.
O mighty rushing stream of Light,
transcendence is my sacred right.

8. Master Paul, you balance all,
the seven rays upon my call.
Master Paul, you paint the sky,
with colors that delight the I.

O Holy Spirit, flow through me,
I am the open door for thee.
O mighty rushing stream of Light,
transcendence is my sacred right.

9. Master Paul, your Presence here,
filling up my inner sphere.
Life is now a sacred flow,
God Love I do on all bestow.

O Holy Spirit, flow through me,
I am the open door for thee.
O mighty rushing stream of Light,
transcendence is my sacred right.

Sealing:

In the name of the Divine Mother, I fully accept that the power of these calls is used to set free the Ma-ter light, so it can outpicture the perfect vision of Christ for my own life, for all people and for the planet. In the name I AM THAT I AM, it is done! Amen.

ABOUT THE AUTHOR

Kim Michaels is a prolific author, having published over 40 books. He has conducted spiritual conferences and workshops in 14 countries, has counseled hundreds of spiritual students and has done numerous radio shows on spiritual topics. Kim has been on the spiritual path since 1976. He has studied a wide variety of spiritual teachings and practiced many techniques for raising consciousness. Since 2002 he has served as a messenger for Jesus and other ascended masters. He has brought forth extensive teachings about the mystical path, many of them available for free on his websites: *www.askrealjesus.com*, *www.ascendedmasteranswers.com*, *www.ascendedmasterlight.com* and *www.transcendencetoolbox.com*. For personal information, visit Kim at *www.KimMichaels.info*.